Can you imagine a
meal without condiments?
NEVER!

No Ketchup on your
hamburger or fries?
NO WAY!

How about condiments
walking off the counter?
WHAAAT!

To
Alexia,
Let's Ketchup soon!
Cheers,
S.A. Wood
11/17

CHEERS!

Meghan, Liza, Peyton, Sebastian, Parker, Jamie, Duke, Matteo, Ruby, Stevie, Charlie, Tatum, Ashdon, Keedin, Blayden, Lundyn, Lennox, Raleigh, Eli, Eva, Finley, Oliver, Avery, Reese, Cameron, Ava, Delaney, Braedon, Emmarie, Alden, Madison, Savanna, Rocco, Brixton, Eloise, Pierce, James, Hazel, Jack, Jojo, Sam, William, Aviana, Macario, Wyatt, Luke, Lena, Ronan, Roisin, Ben, Emily, Crosby, Brig, Arden, Jack, Gray, Whit, David, Julianna, Matthew, Rayne, Lyric, Jacob, Cora, Asa, Grace, Faith, Georgia and

FUTURE CONDIMENTOURS

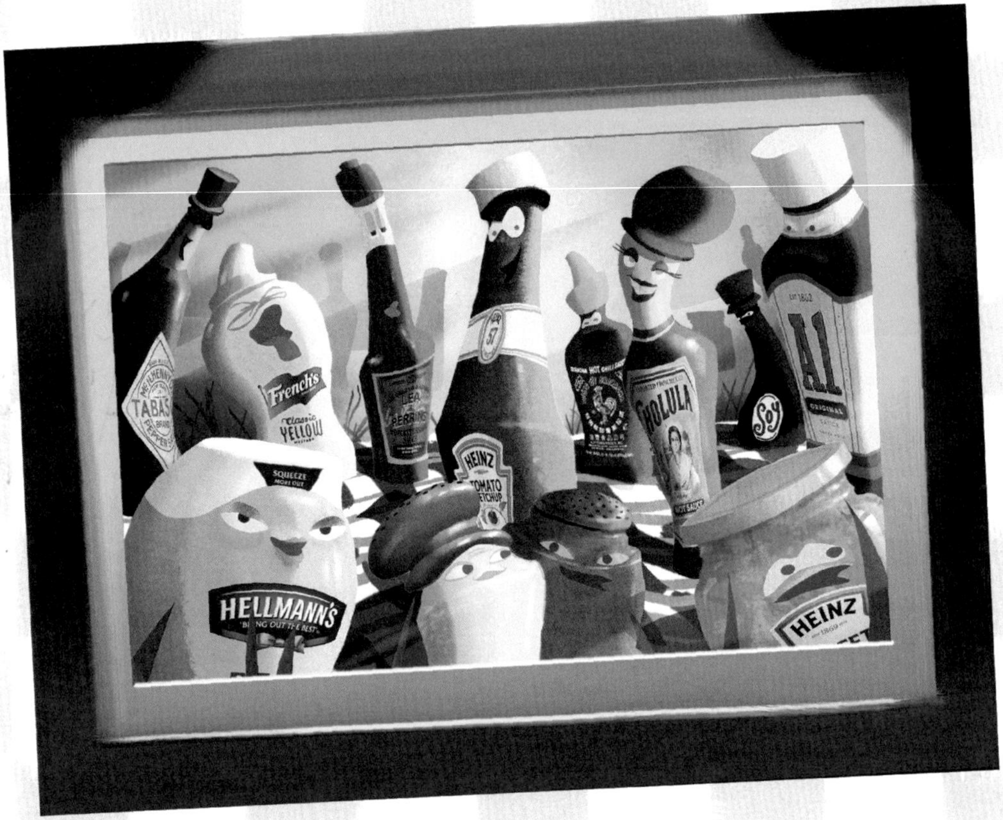
French's
Classic YELLOW
HEINZ TOMATO KETCHUP
A1
Soy
SQUEEZE
HELLMANN'S
HEINZ

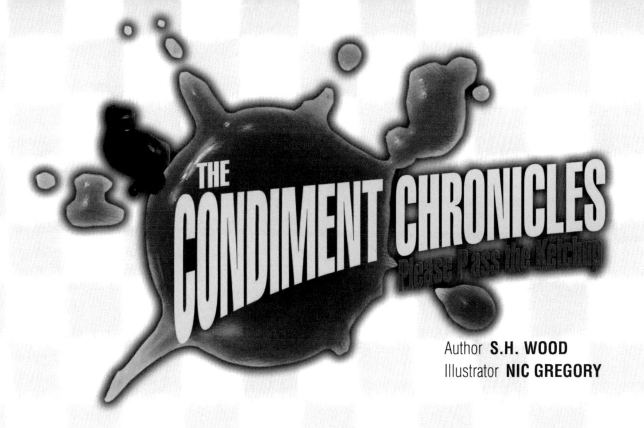

THE CONDIMENT CHRONICLES
Please Pass the Ketchup

Author **S.H. WOOD**
Illustrator **NIC GREGORY**

Many thanks to the following companies for their kind permission in allowing reproduction of their Intellectual Property for each individual condiment represented in this book:

Kraft Heinz: Heinz ketchup, Heinz relish, Lea & Perrins Worcestershire sauce, A.1. sauce.
Unilever: Hellmann's® Mayonnaise reproduced with kind permission of Unilever PLC and group companies.
McIlhenny Company: TABASCO®, the Diamond and Bottle Logos, are trademarks of McIlhenny Company, registered in the U.S. And other countries.
Reckitt Benckiser: French's® Classic Yellow Mustard
Jose Cuervo: Cholula® Hot Sauce
Huy Fong Foods: Sriracha Hot Chili Sauce

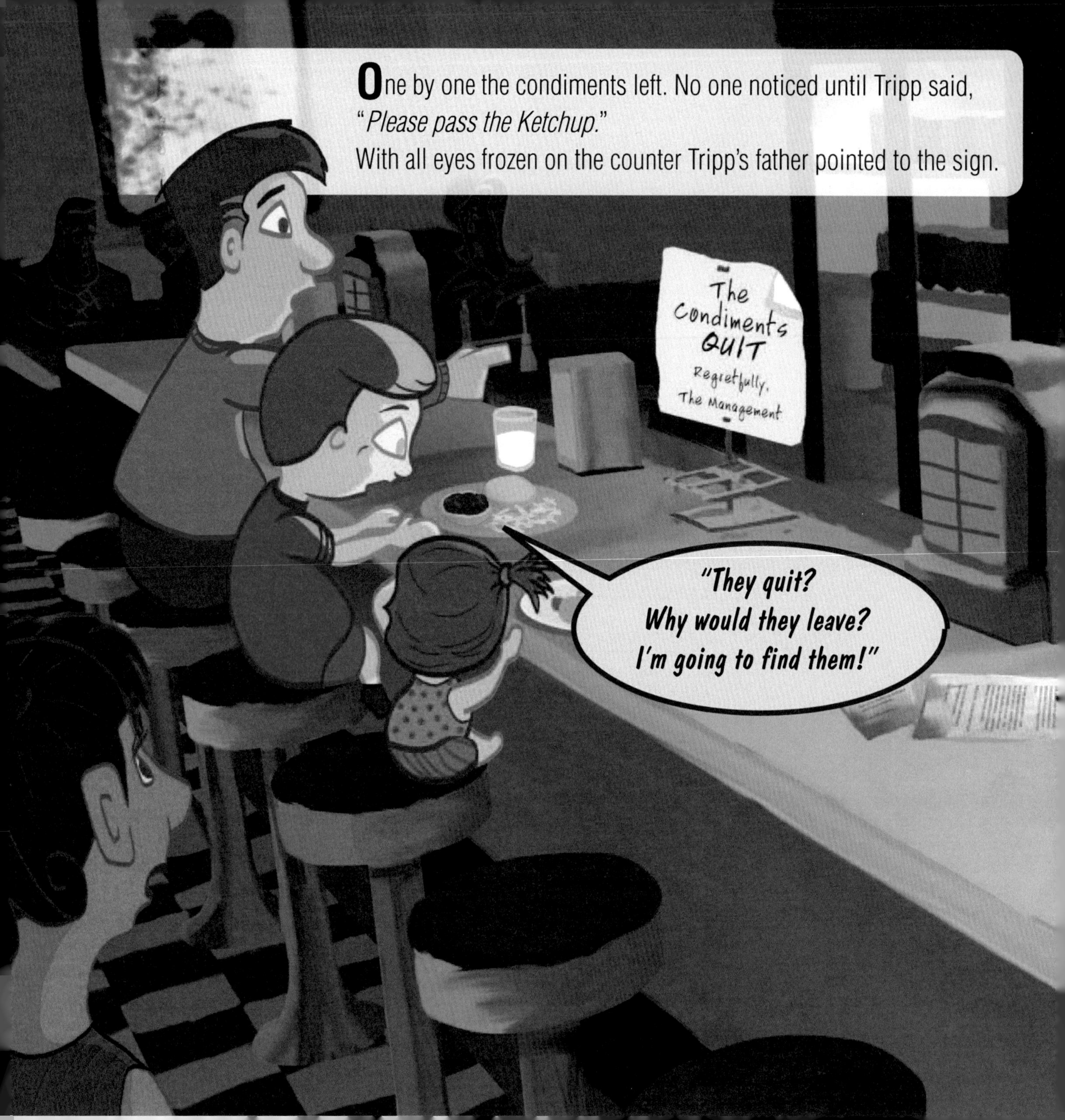
One by one the condiments left. No one noticed until Tripp said,
"*Please pass the Ketchup.*"
With all eyes frozen on the counter Tripp's father pointed to the sign.
The Condiments QUIT
Regretfully, The Management
"They quit? Why would they leave? I'm going to find them!"

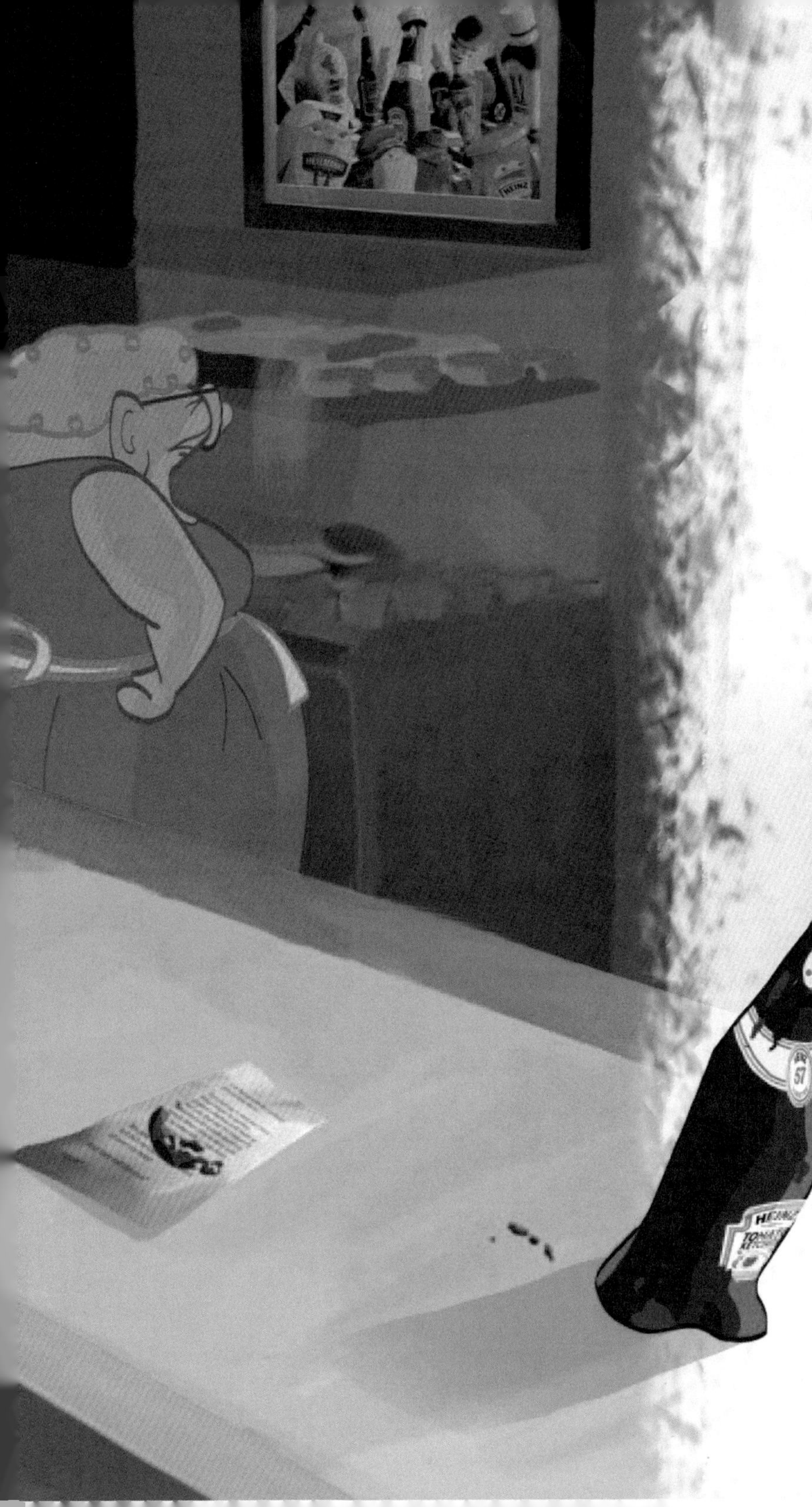

Ketchup, Mayo, Mustard,
Relish, Tabasco® Sauce, Salt and
Pepper, Hot, Sweet, and Savory
Sauces, Sugars, Salsas, Jams, and
Jellies … sadly, there were many
more like Teriyaki and
Worcestershire standing on
alert; off-counter only to
appear upon request.

Papers on the counter told the
whole story; detailed conversations
of complaints of abuse, misuse,
prejudice, discrimination,
and more.

Ketchup was the first to speak out ...

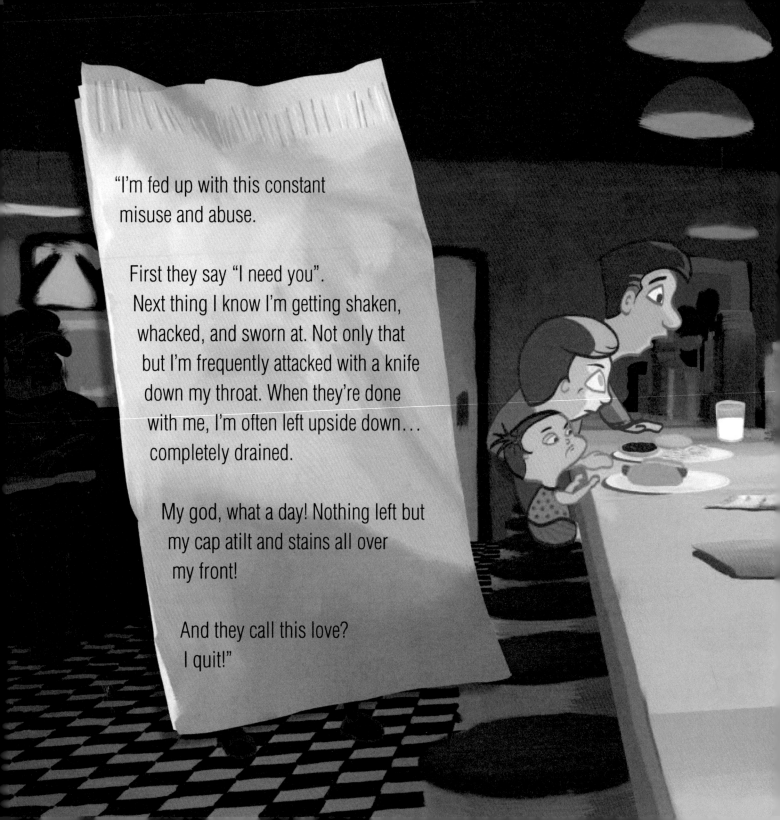

"I'm fed up with this constant
misuse and abuse.

First they say "I need you".
Next thing I know I'm getting shaken,
whacked, and sworn at. Not only that
but I'm frequently attacked with a knife
down my throat. When they're done
with me, I'm often left upside down…
completely drained.

My god, what a day! Nothing left but
my cap atilt and stains all over
my front!

And they call this love?
I quit!"

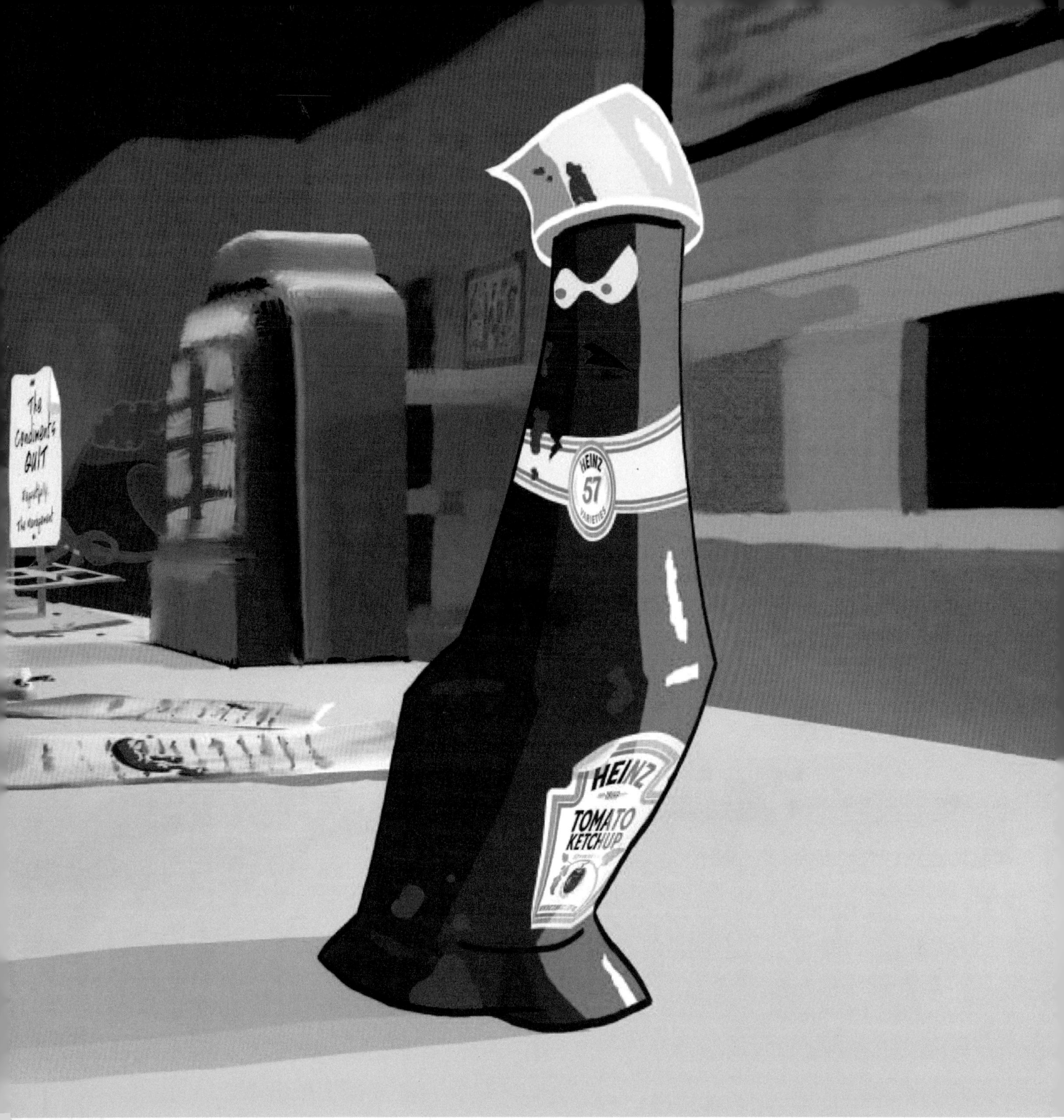
The Condiment's GUIT
HEINZ 57 VARIETIES
HEINZ
TOMATO KETCHUP

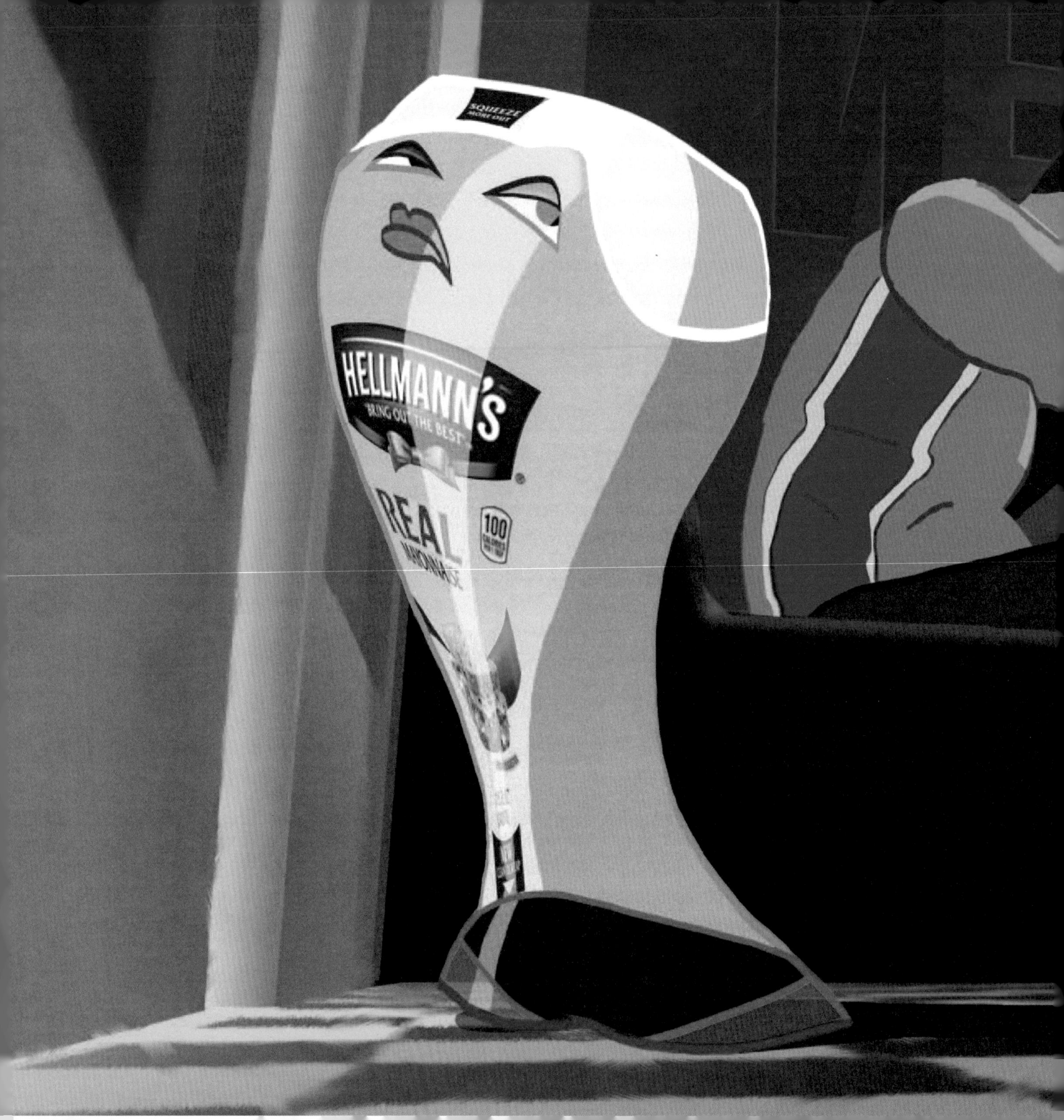
SQUEEZE
MORE OUT
HELLMANN'S
BRING OUT THE BEST
REAL

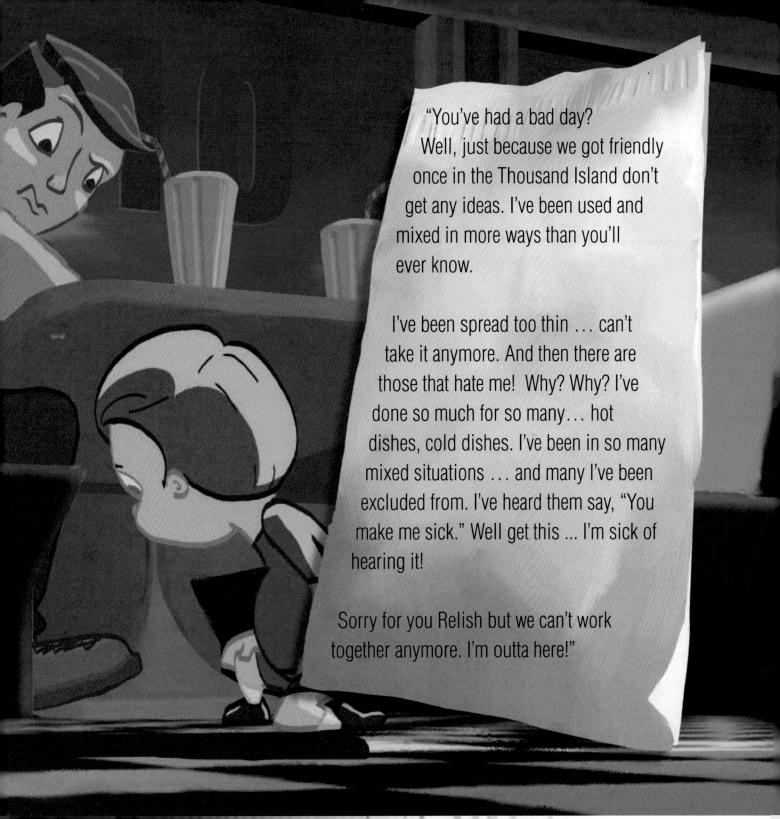

"You've had a bad day? Well, just because we got friendly once in the Thousand Island don't get any ideas. I've been used and mixed in more ways than you'll ever know.

I've been spread too thin … can't take it anymore. And then there are those that hate me! Why? Why? I've done so much for so many… hot dishes, cold dishes. I've been in so many mixed situations … and many I've been excluded from. I've heard them say, "You make me sick." Well get this … I'm sick of hearing it!

Sorry for you Relish but we can't work together anymore. I'm outta here!"

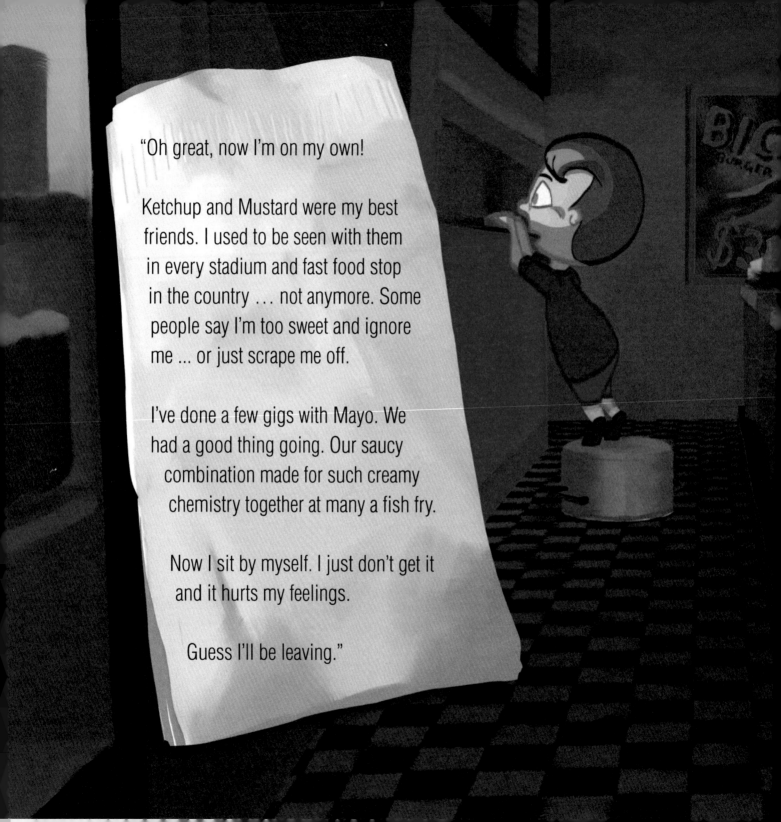

"Oh great, now I'm on my own!

Ketchup and Mustard were my best friends. I used to be seen with them in every stadium and fast food stop in the country … not anymore. Some people say I'm too sweet and ignore me … or just scrape me off.

I've done a few gigs with Mayo. We had a good thing going. Our saucy combination made for such creamy chemistry together at many a fish fry.

Now I sit by myself. I just don't get it and it hurts my feelings.

Guess I'll be leaving."

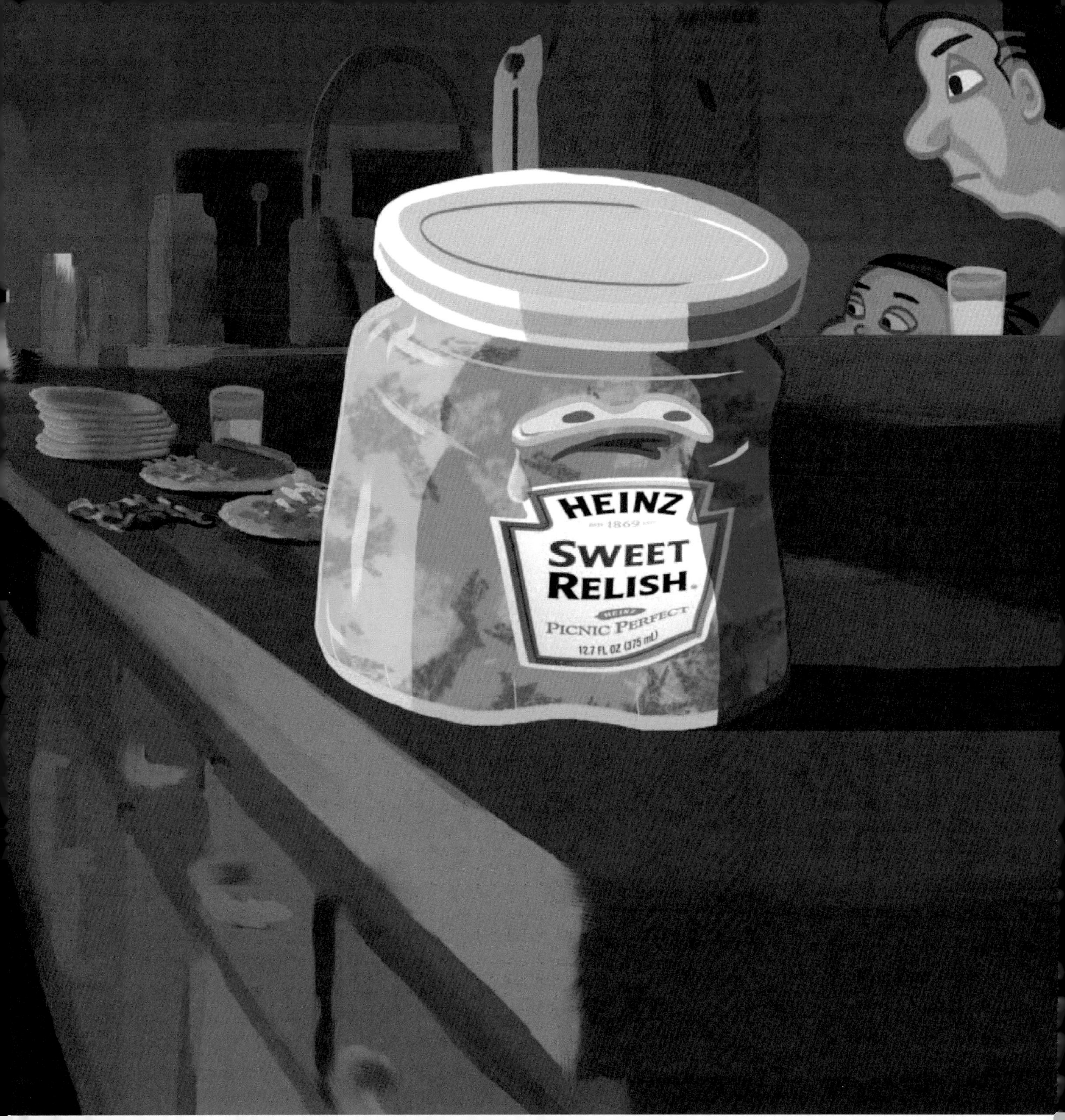
HEINZ
1869
SWEET
RELISH
HEINZ
PICNIC PERFECT
12.7 FL OZ (375 mL)

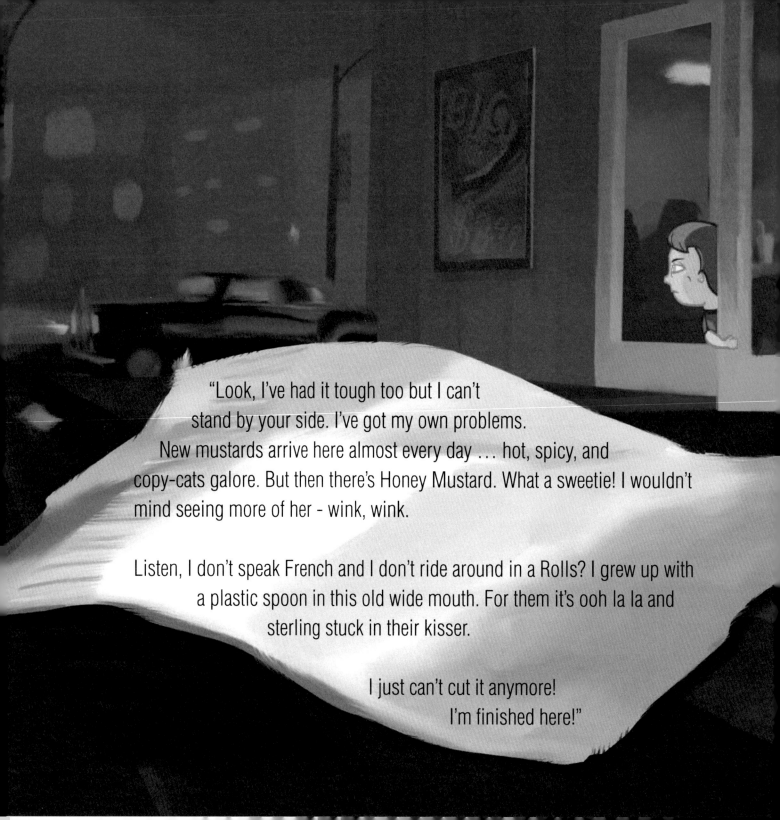

"Look, I've had it tough too but I can't
stand by your side. I've got my own problems.
New mustards arrive here almost every day … hot, spicy, and
copy-cats galore. But then there's Honey Mustard. What a sweetie! I wouldn't
mind seeing more of her - wink, wink.

Listen, I don't speak French and I don't ride around in a Rolls? I grew up with
a plastic spoon in this old wide mouth. For them it's ooh la la and
sterling stuck in their kisser.

I just can't cut it anymore!
I'm finished here!"

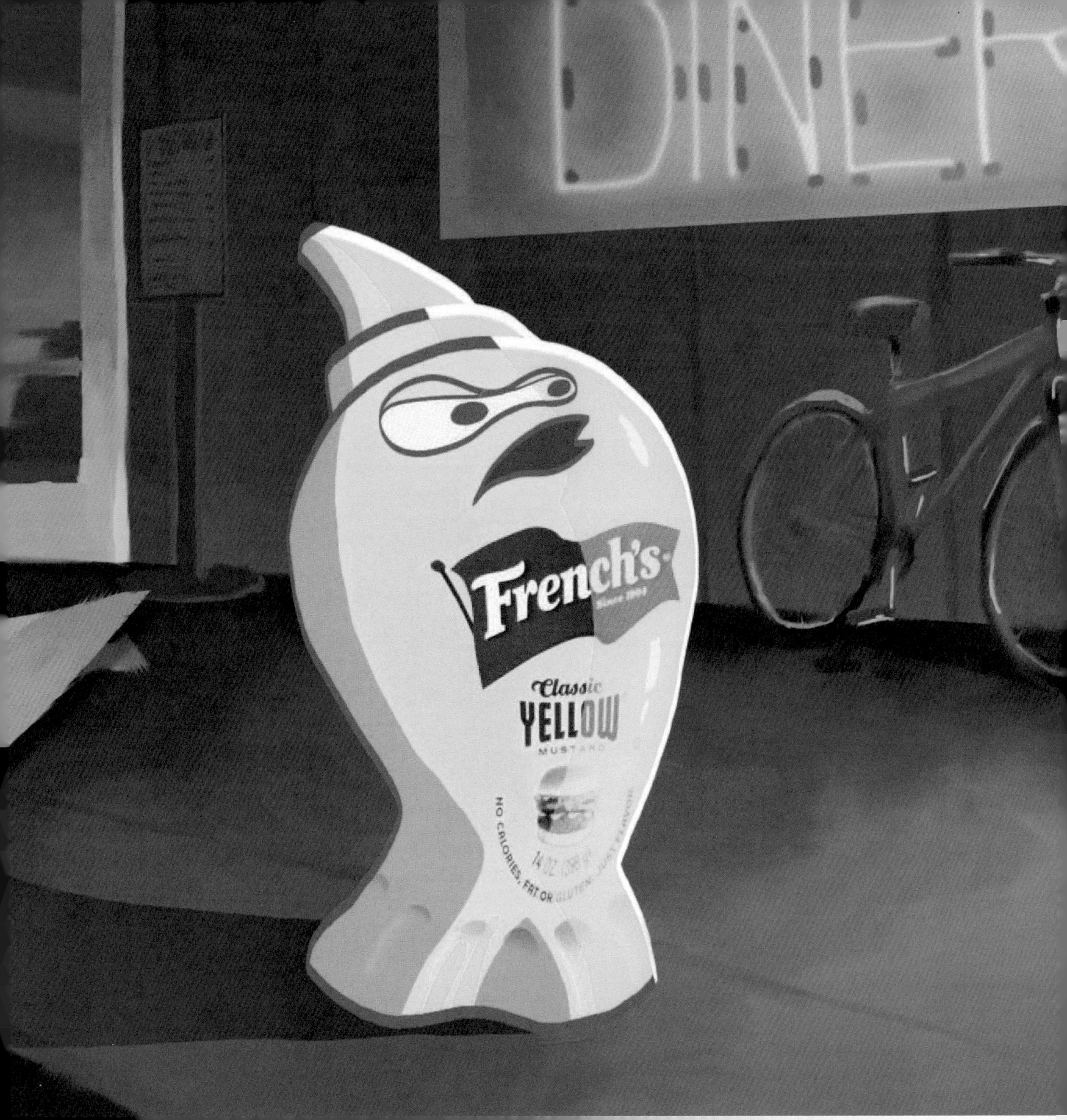
DINE
French's
Classic
YELLOW
MUSTARD
NO CALORIES, FAT OR GLUTEN.

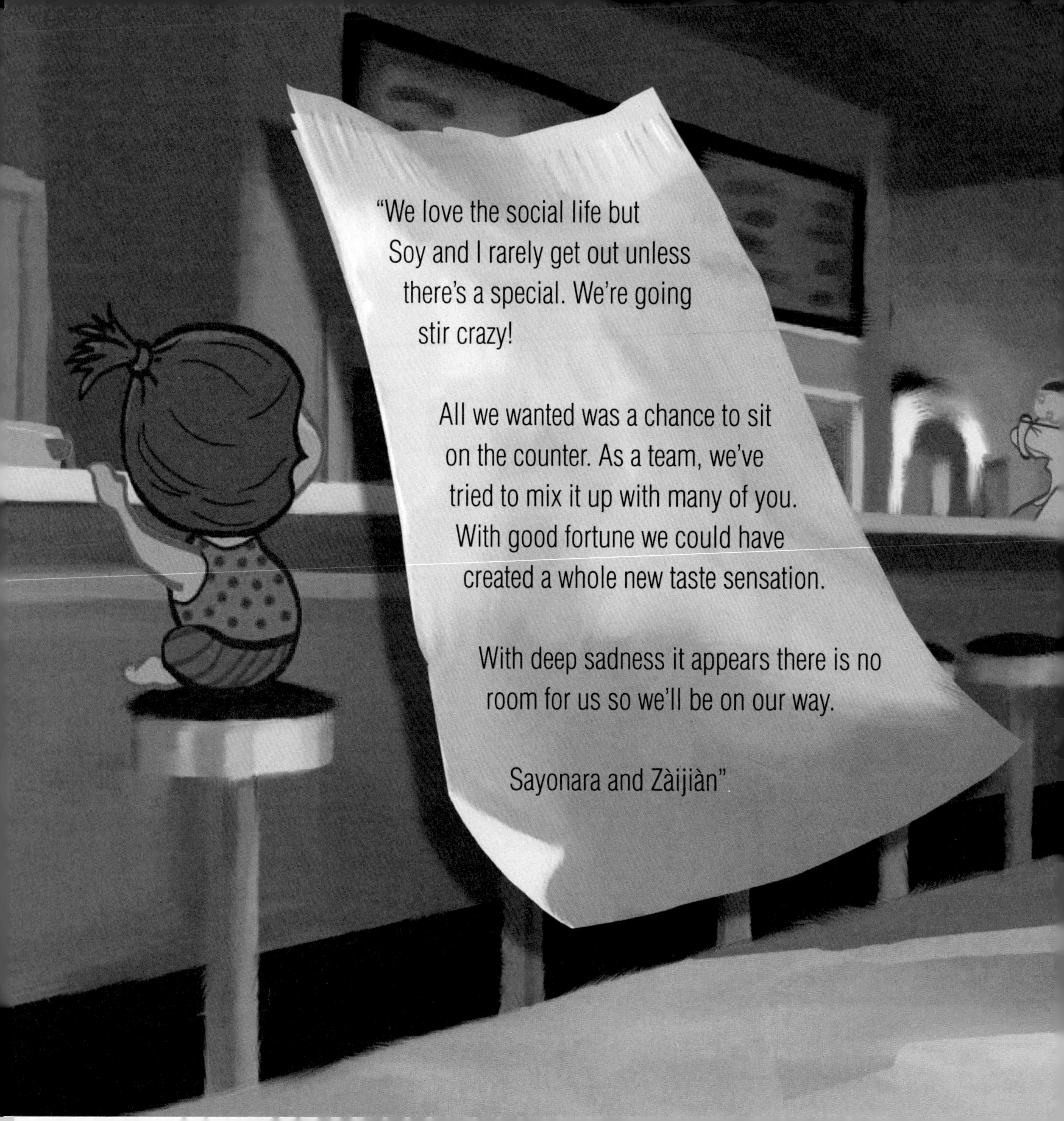

"We love the social life but
Soy and I rarely get out unless
there's a special. We're going
stir crazy!

All we wanted was a chance to sit
on the counter. As a team, we've
tried to mix it up with many of you.
With good fortune we could have
created a whole new taste sensation.

With deep sadness it appears there is no
room for us so we'll be on our way.

Sayonara and Zàijiàn".

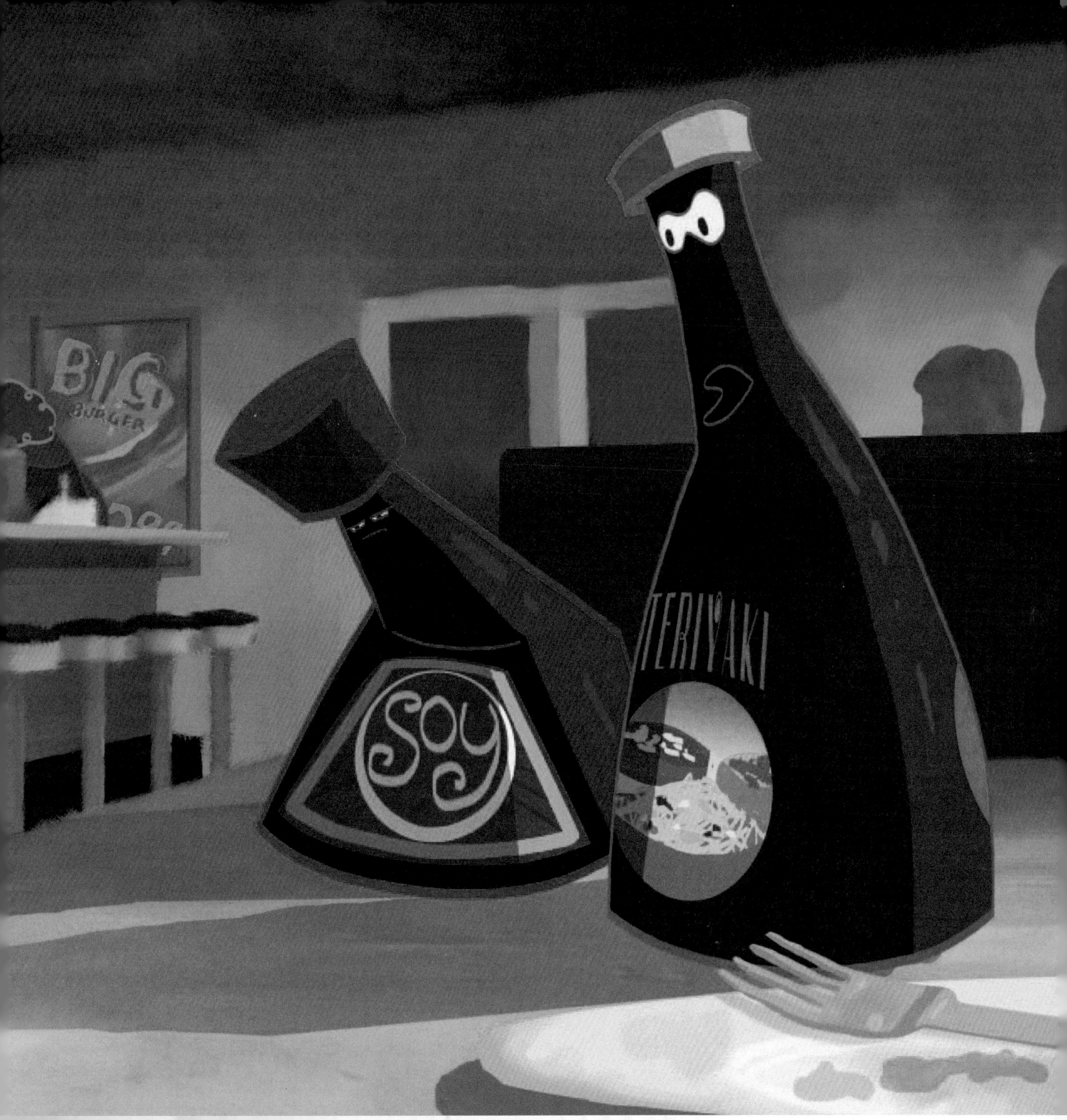
BIG
BURGER
SOY
TERIYAKI

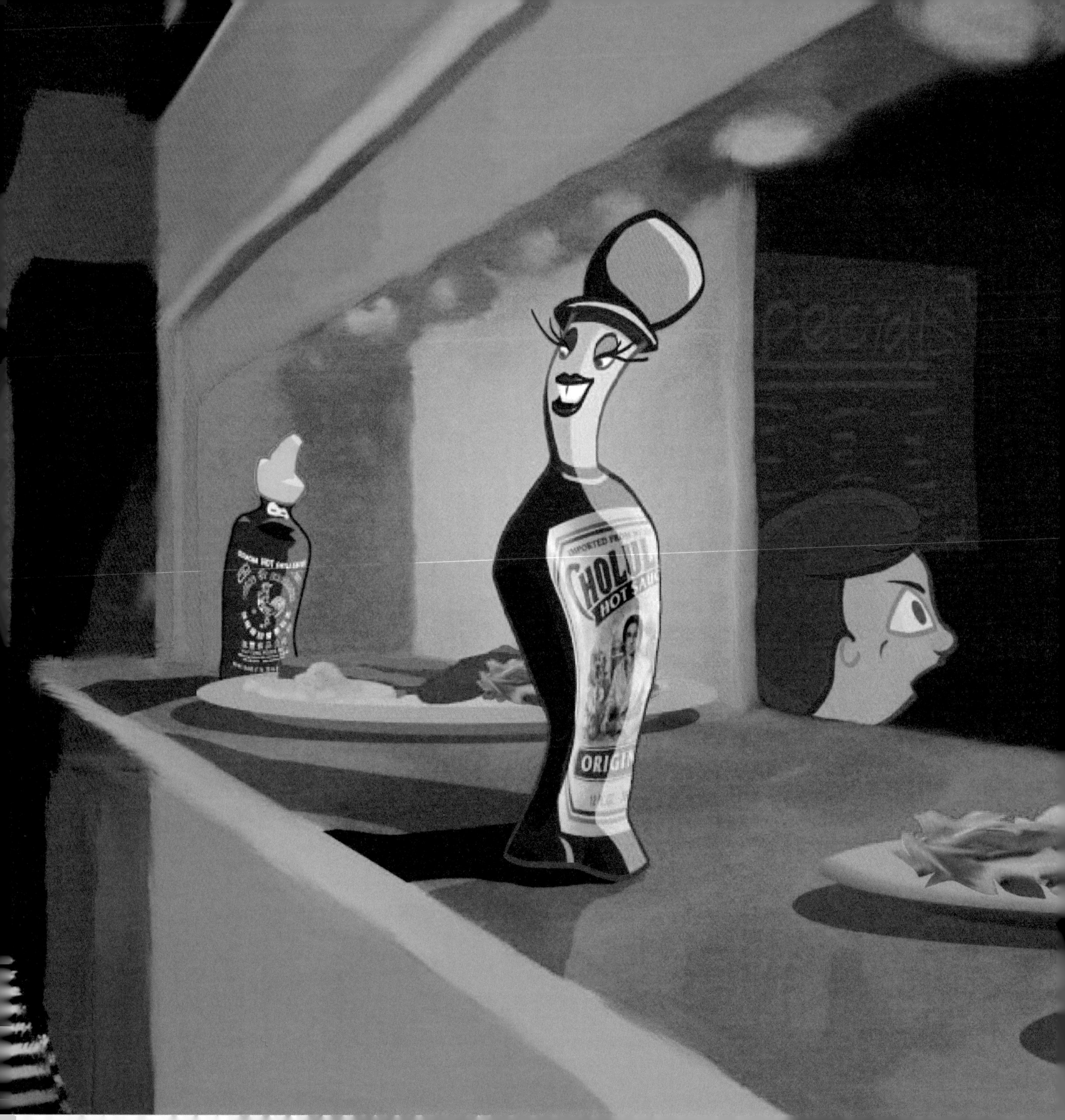

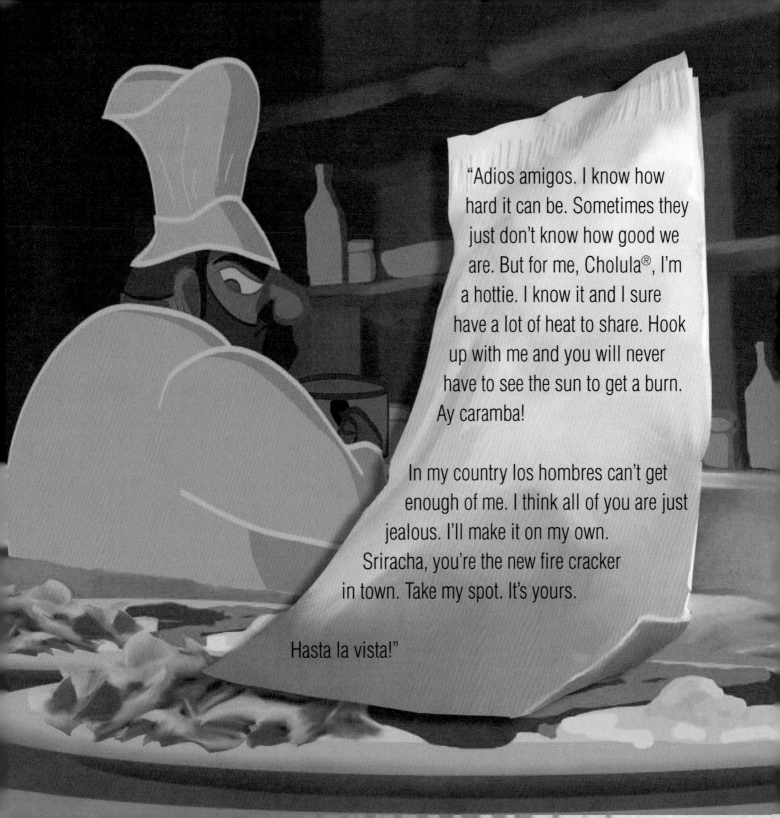

"Adios amigos. I know how hard it can be. Sometimes they just don't know how good we are. But for me, Cholula®, I'm a hottie. I know it and I sure have a lot of heat to share. Hook up with me and you will never have to see the sun to get a burn. Ay caramba!

In my country los hombres can't get enough of me. I think all of you are just jealous. I'll make it on my own. Sriracha, you're the new fire cracker in town. Take my spot. It's yours.

Hasta la vista!"

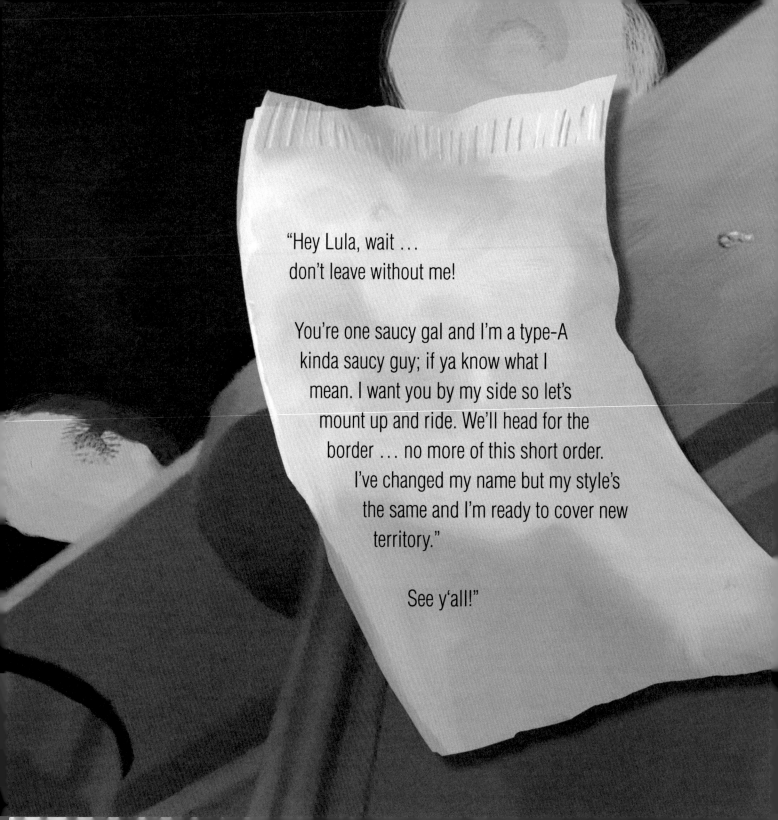

"Hey Lula, wait …
don't leave without me!

You're one saucy gal and I'm a type-A
kinda saucy guy; if ya know what I
mean. I want you by my side so let's
mount up and ride. We'll head for the
border … no more of this short order.
I've changed my name but my style's
the same and I'm ready to cover new
territory."

See y'all!"

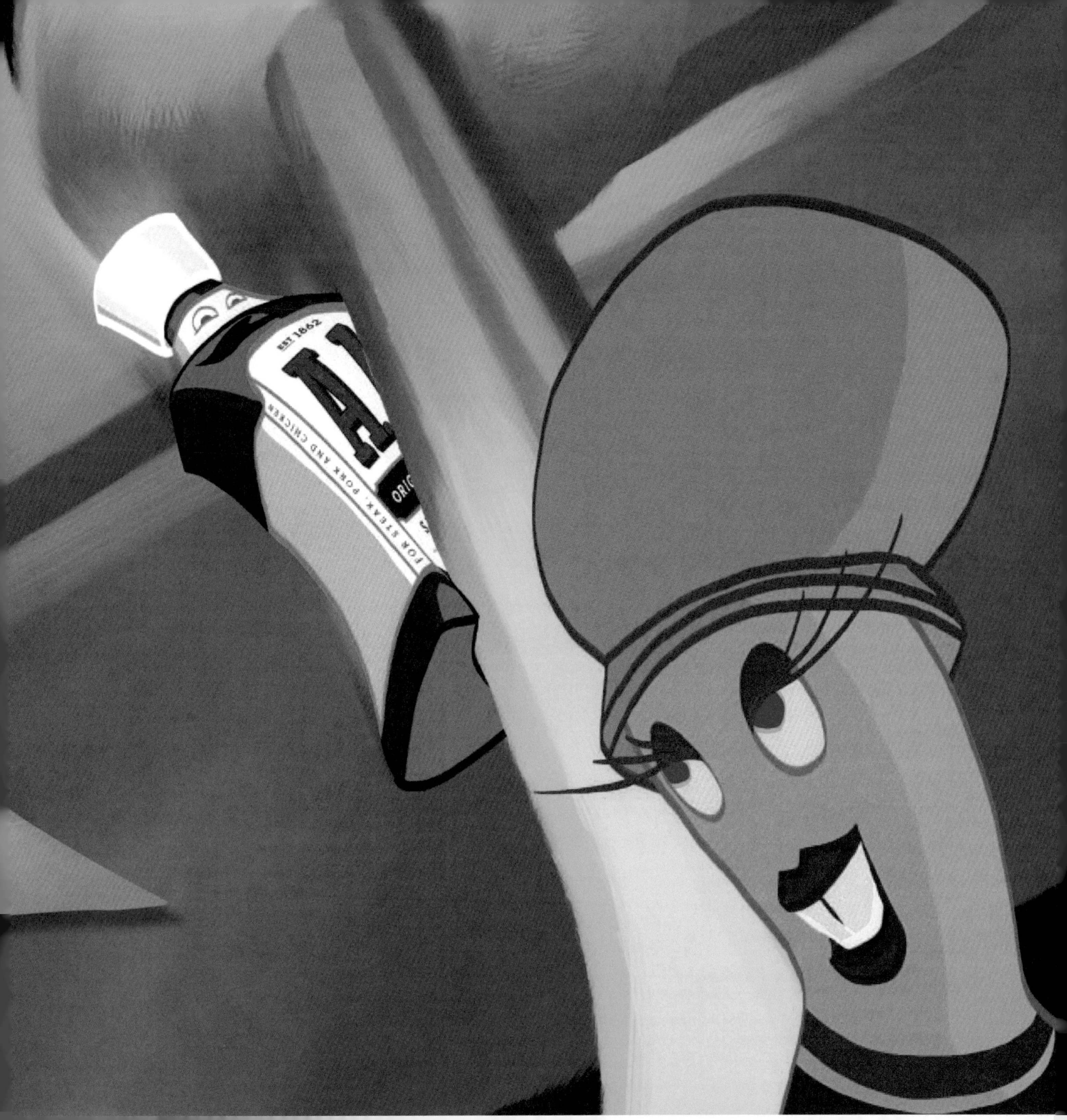
EST 1862
FOR STEAK, PORK AND CHICKEN

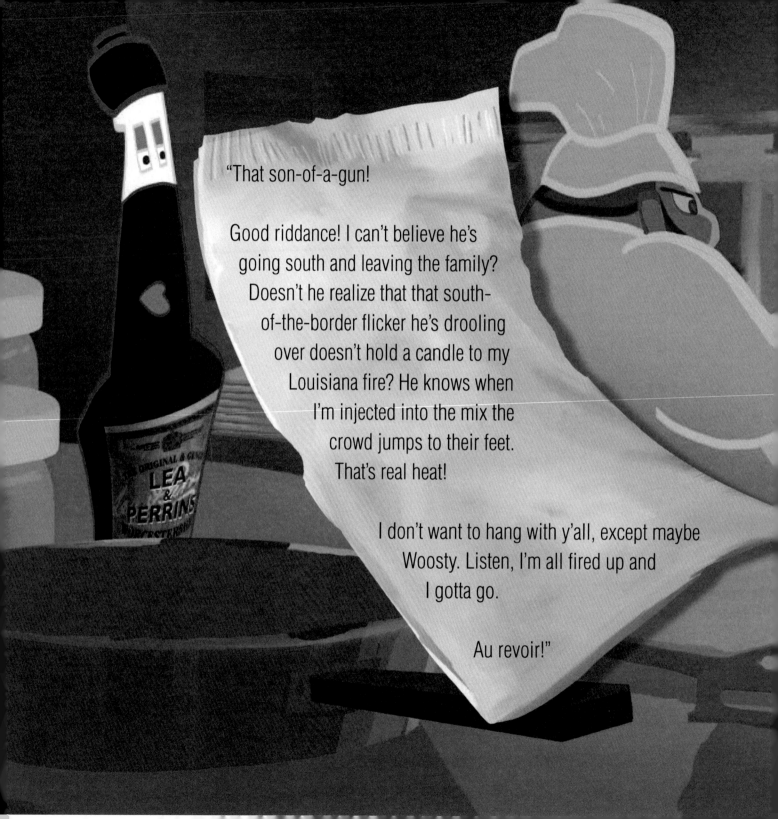

"That son-of-a-gun!

Good riddance! I can't believe he's going south and leaving the family? Doesn't he realize that that south-of-the-border flicker he's drooling over doesn't hold a candle to my Louisiana fire? He knows when I'm injected into the mix the crowd jumps to their feet. That's real heat!

I don't want to hang with y'all, except maybe Woosty. Listen, I'm all fired up and I gotta go.

Au revoir!"

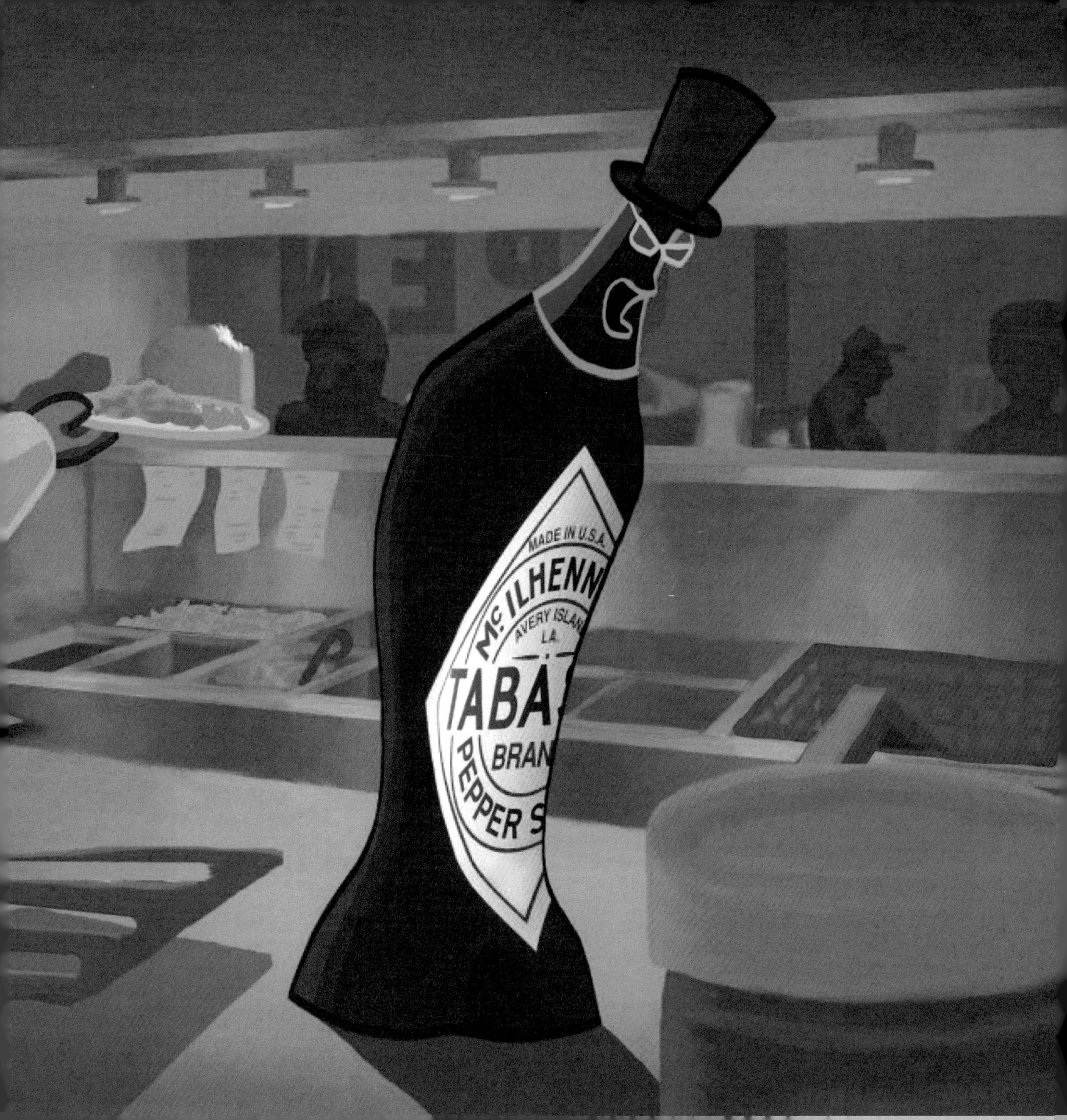
MADE IN U.S.A.
LA.
PEPPER

"Gosh, you all are leaving?

Since the two of us hooked up
together many, many years ago,
before you were even a glimmer in
our eyes, you don't know how hard
it's been. Together, we pound the
counter every day. It's a rough life and
we're all shook up. You got it … one
minute we're up and one minute we're
down. It's a real grind. Without family
standing by our side we'll never get a fair
shake and these days we know we can't shake
it on our own.

Just you wait … they're going to miss us when
we're gone!

Good bye."

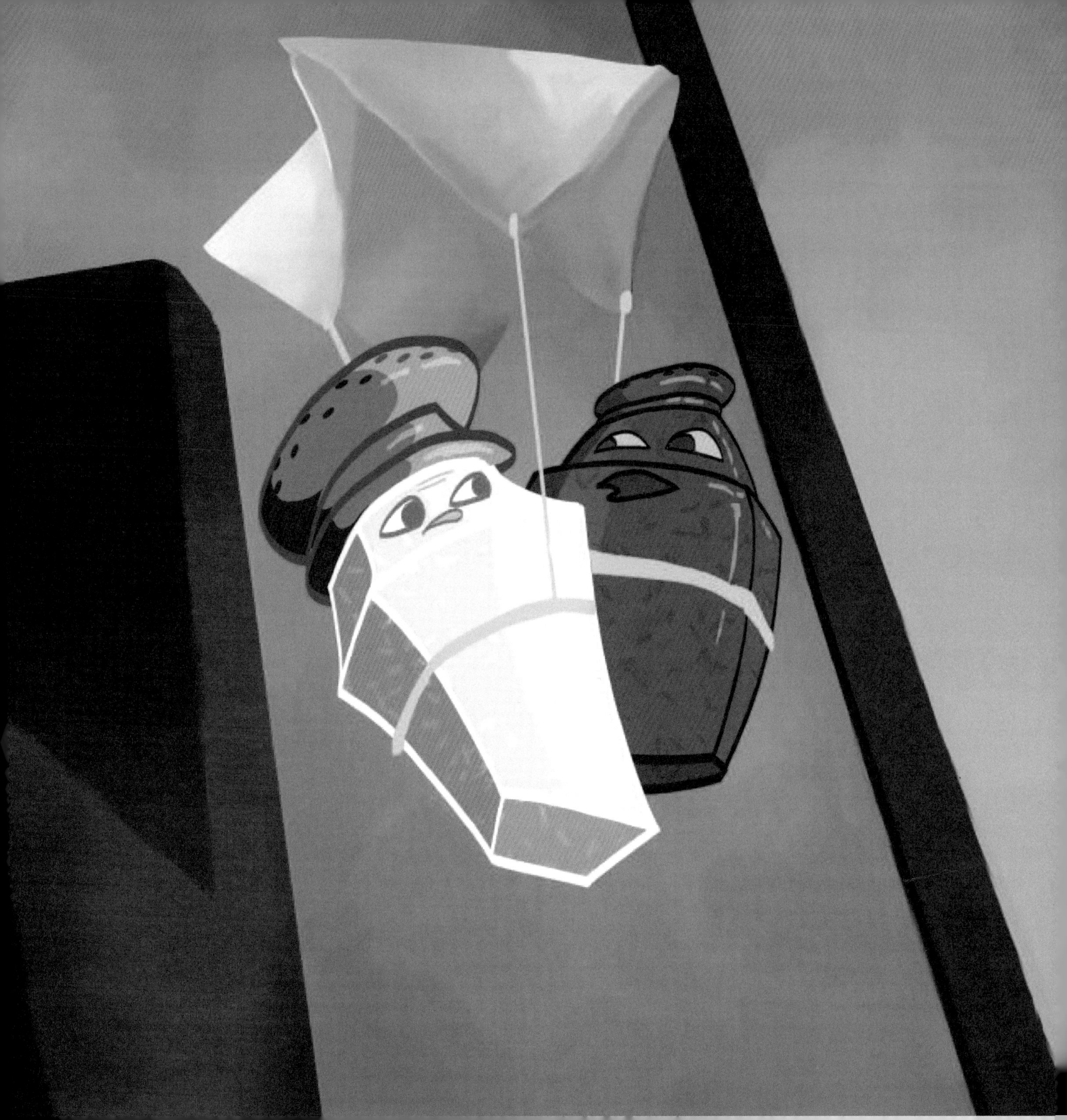

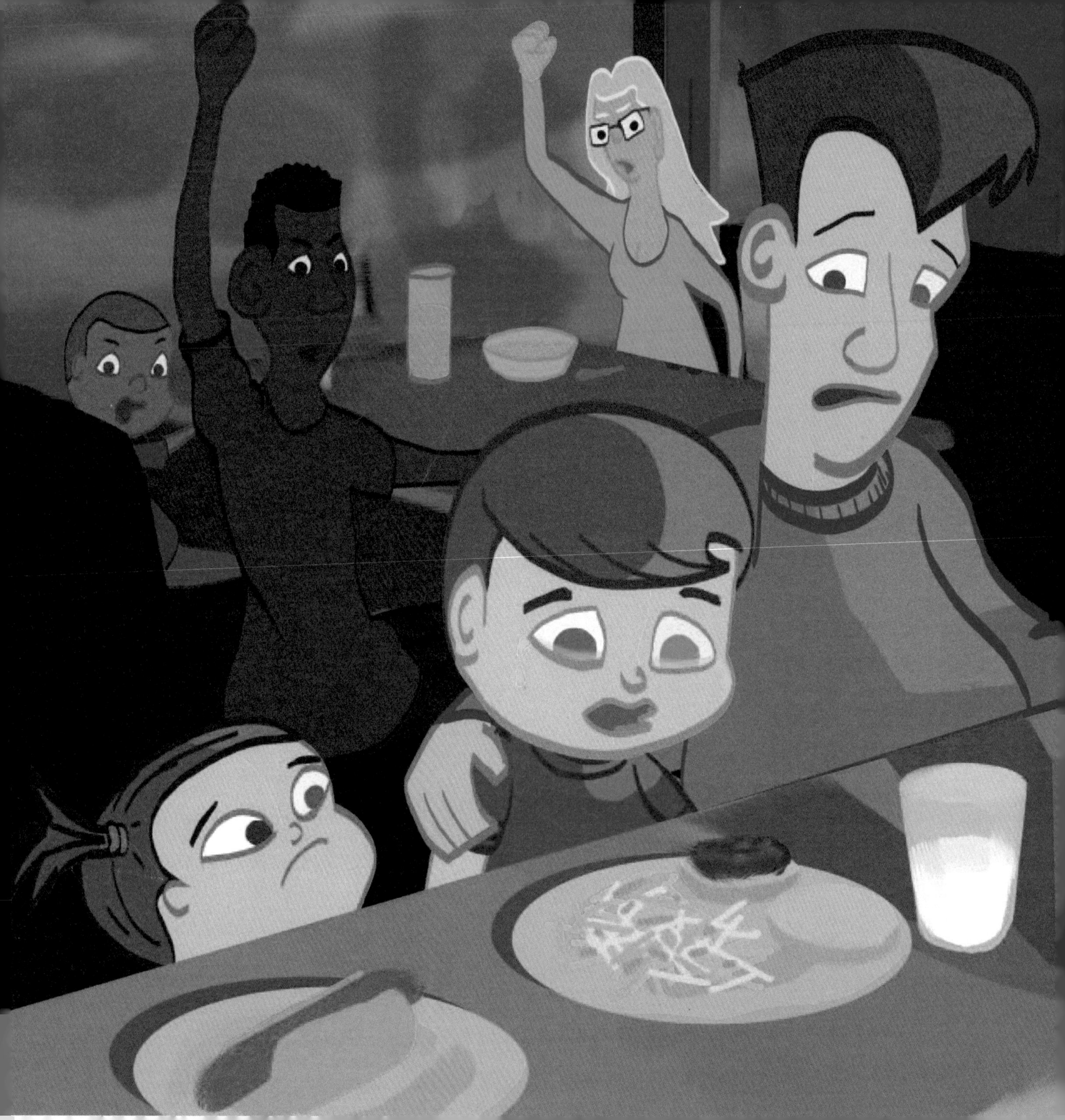

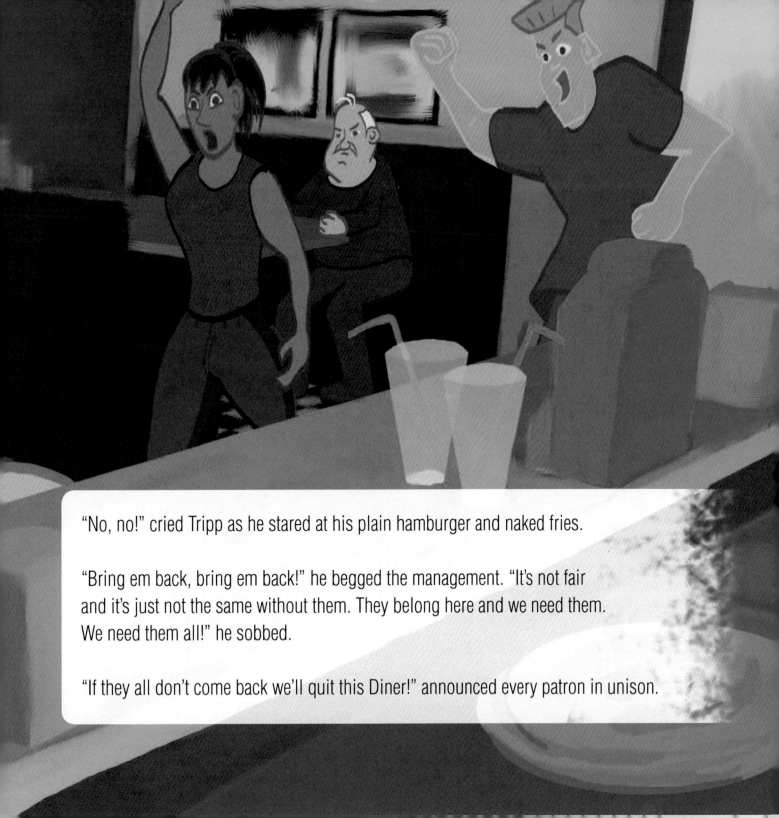

"No, no!" cried Tripp as he stared at his plain hamburger and naked fries.

"Bring em back, bring em back!" he begged the management. "It's not fair and it's just not the same without them. They belong here and we need them. We need them all!" he sobbed.

"If they all don't come back we'll quit this Diner!" announced every patron in unison.

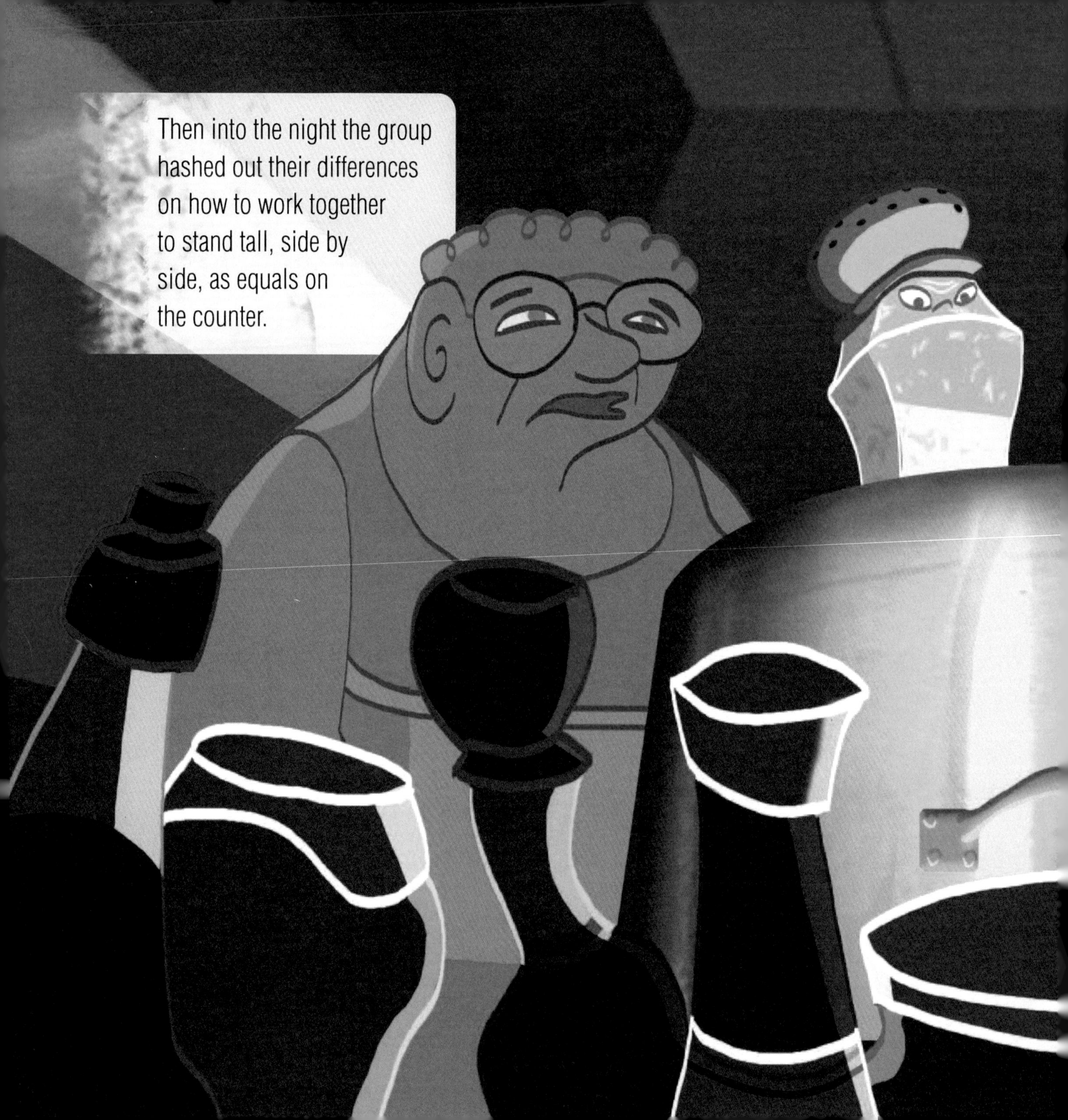

Then into the night the group hashed out their differences on how to work together to stand tall, side by side, as equals on the counter.

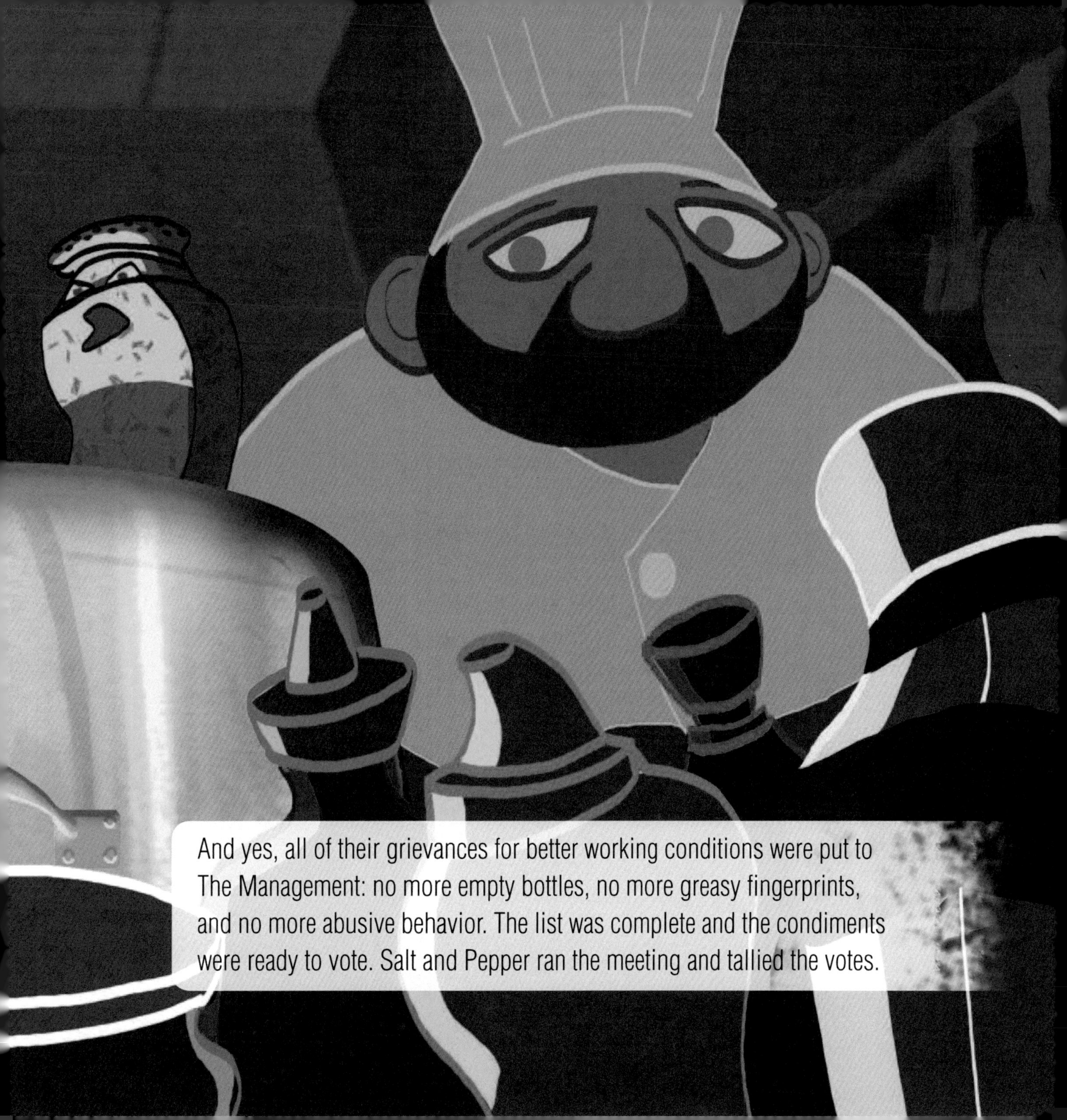

And yes, all of their grievances for better working conditions were put to The Management: no more empty bottles, no more greasy fingerprints, and no more abusive behavior. The list was complete and the condiments were ready to vote. Salt and Pepper ran the meeting and tallied the votes.

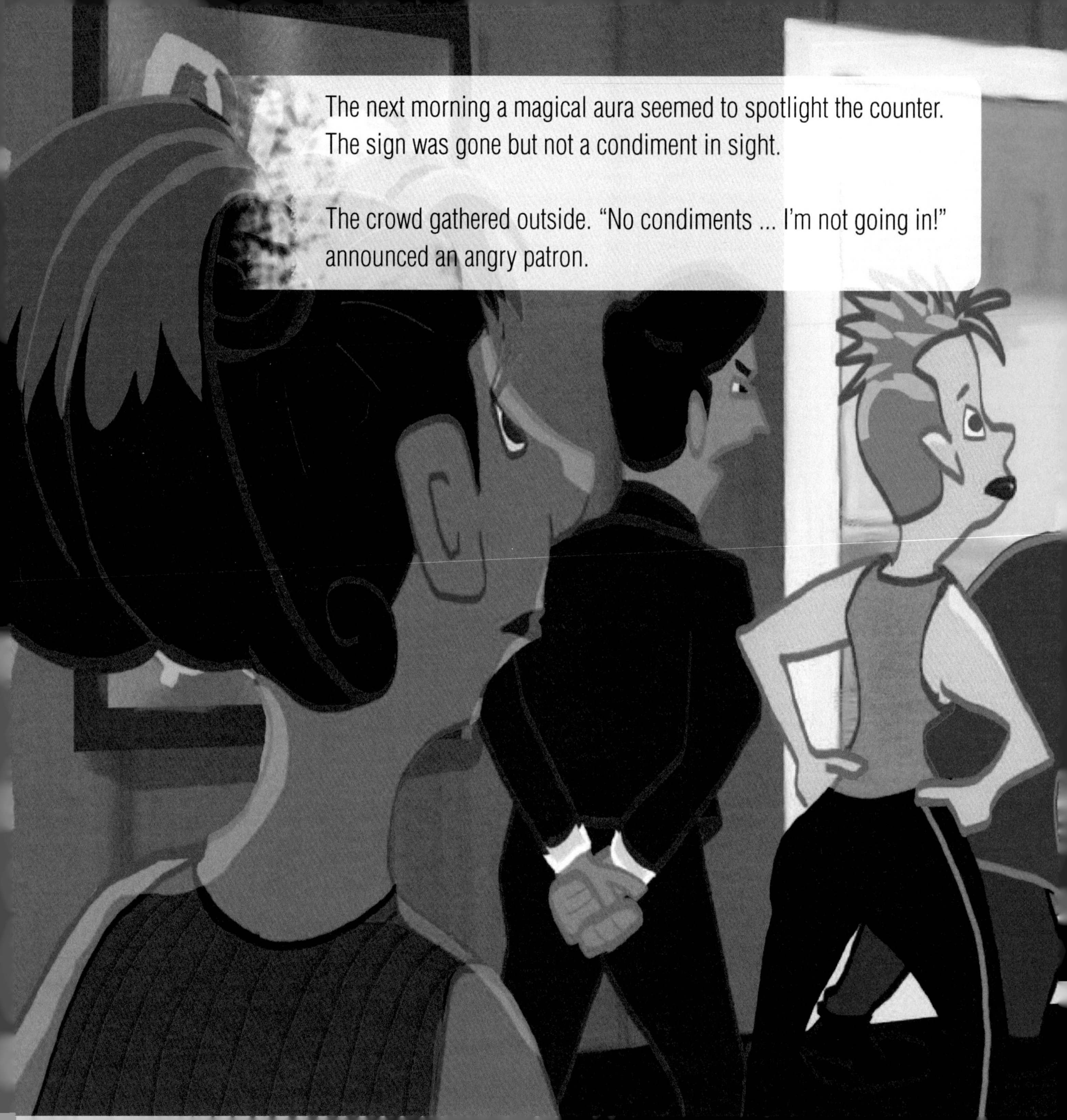

The next morning a magical aura seemed to spotlight the counter. The sign was gone but not a condiment in sight.

The crowd gathered outside. “No condiments ... I’m not going in!” announced an angry patron.

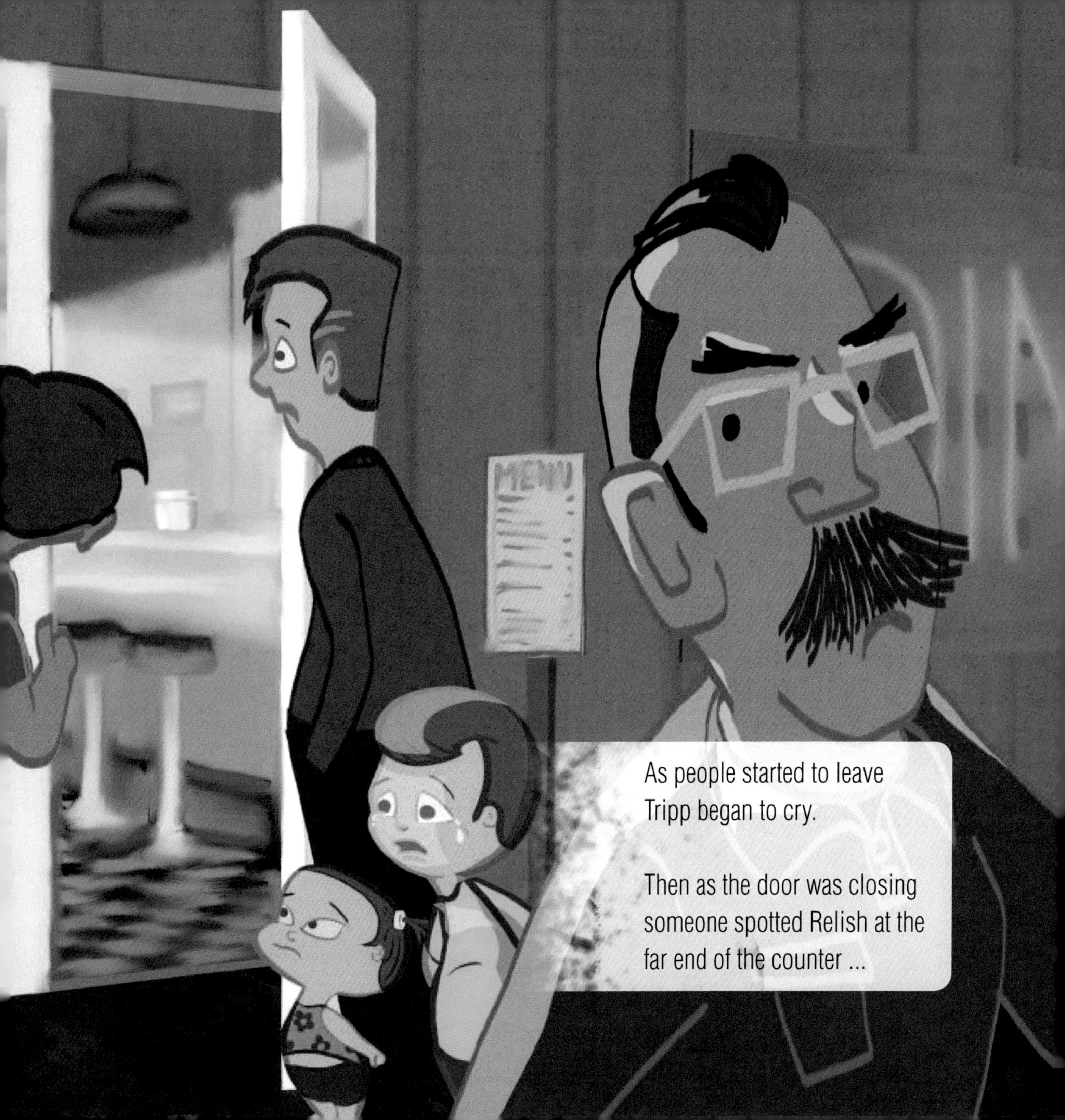
MENU

As people started to leave Tripp began to cry.

Then as the door was closing someone spotted Relish at the far end of the counter ...

With orderly precision a parade of condiments, dressed in their shiny clean bottles, proudly filed out behind Relish. In disbelief the cheering patrons flooded into The Diner.

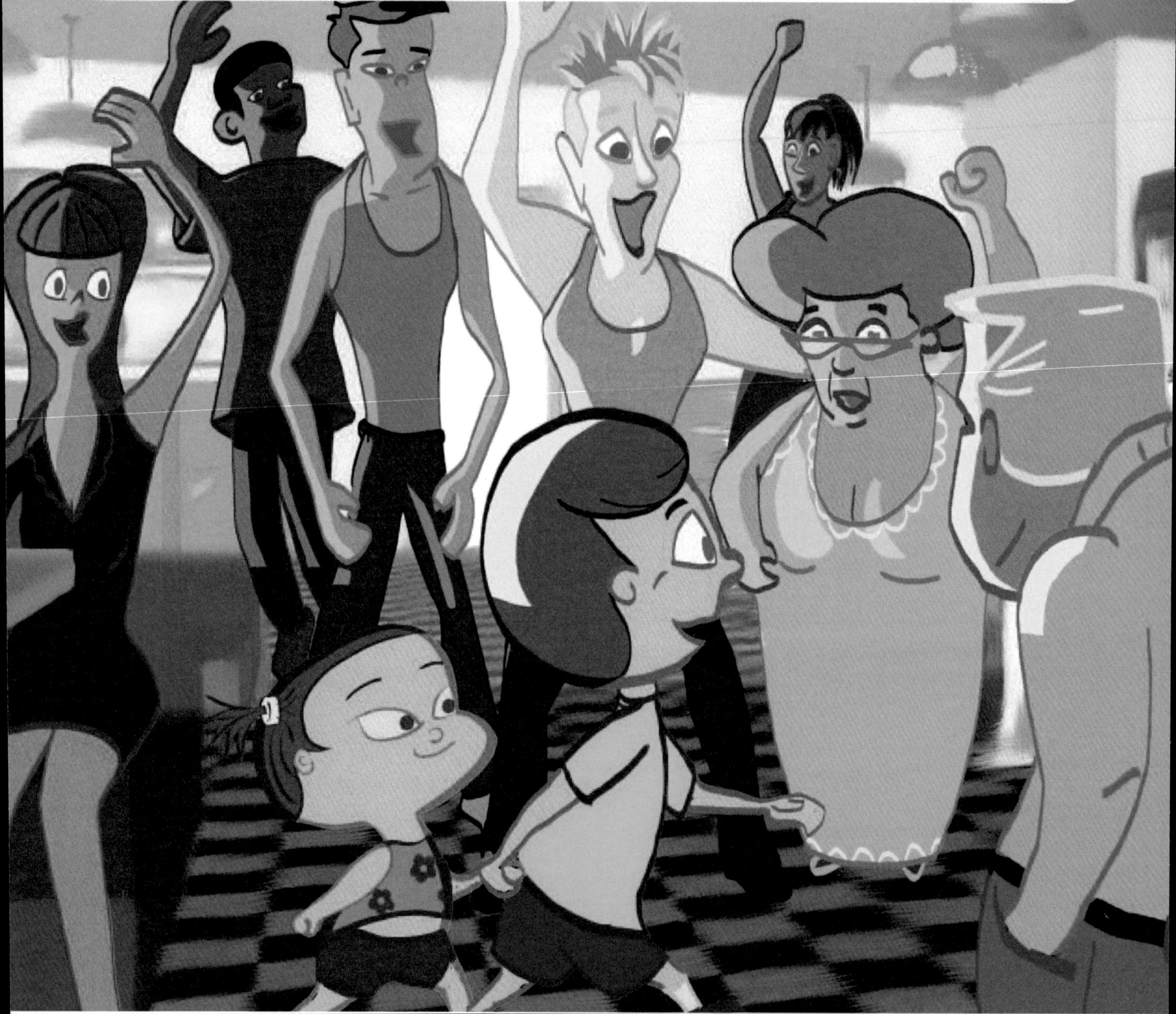

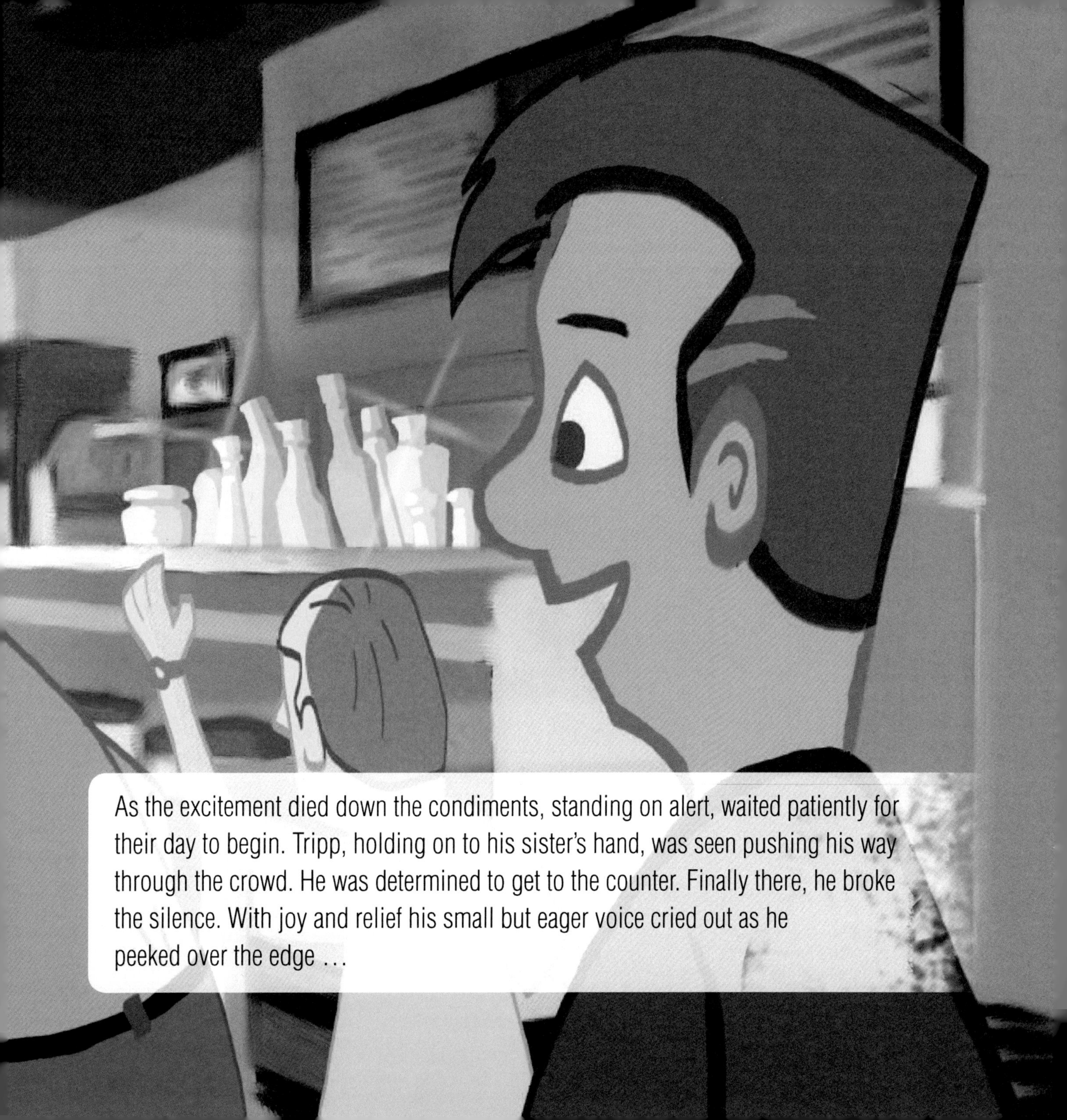

As the excitement died down the condiments, standing on alert, waited patiently for their day to begin. Tripp, holding on to his sister's hand, was seen pushing his way through the crowd. He was determined to get to the counter. Finally there, he broke the silence. With joy and relief his small but eager voice cried out as he peeked over the edge …

THEY'RE BACK!

Someone ... please pass me the Ketchup!"

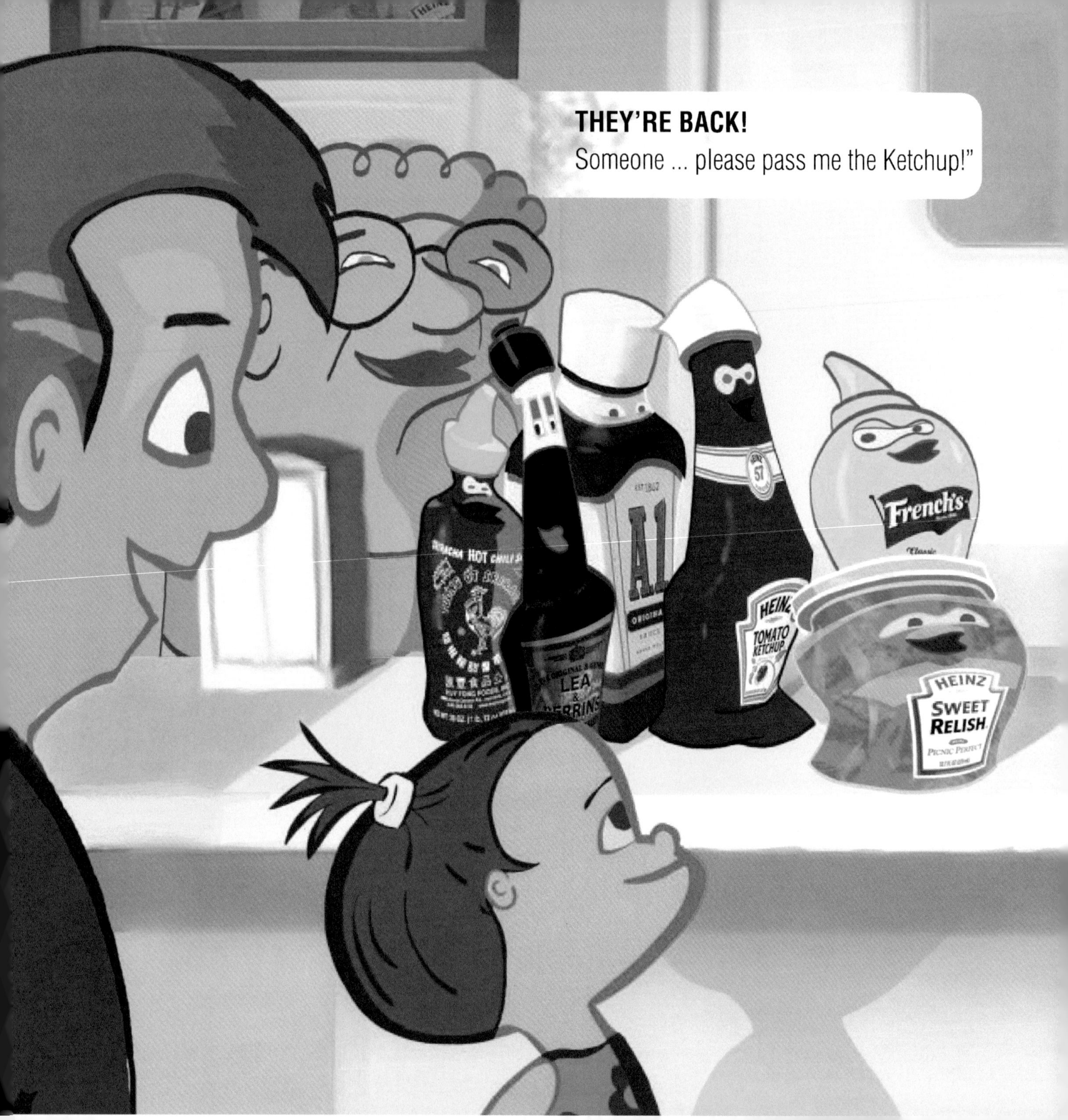

French's
A1
LEA & PERRINS
HEINZ
TOMATO KETCHUP
HEINZ
SWEET RELISH

Suddenly, there was perfect pandemonium - *Thanks, I'll take a little Mustard. Anyone seen Cholula®. Please pass the Salt and Pepper. Yes, Mayo on that please. Thanks, I could use a little Tabasco® Sauce…*

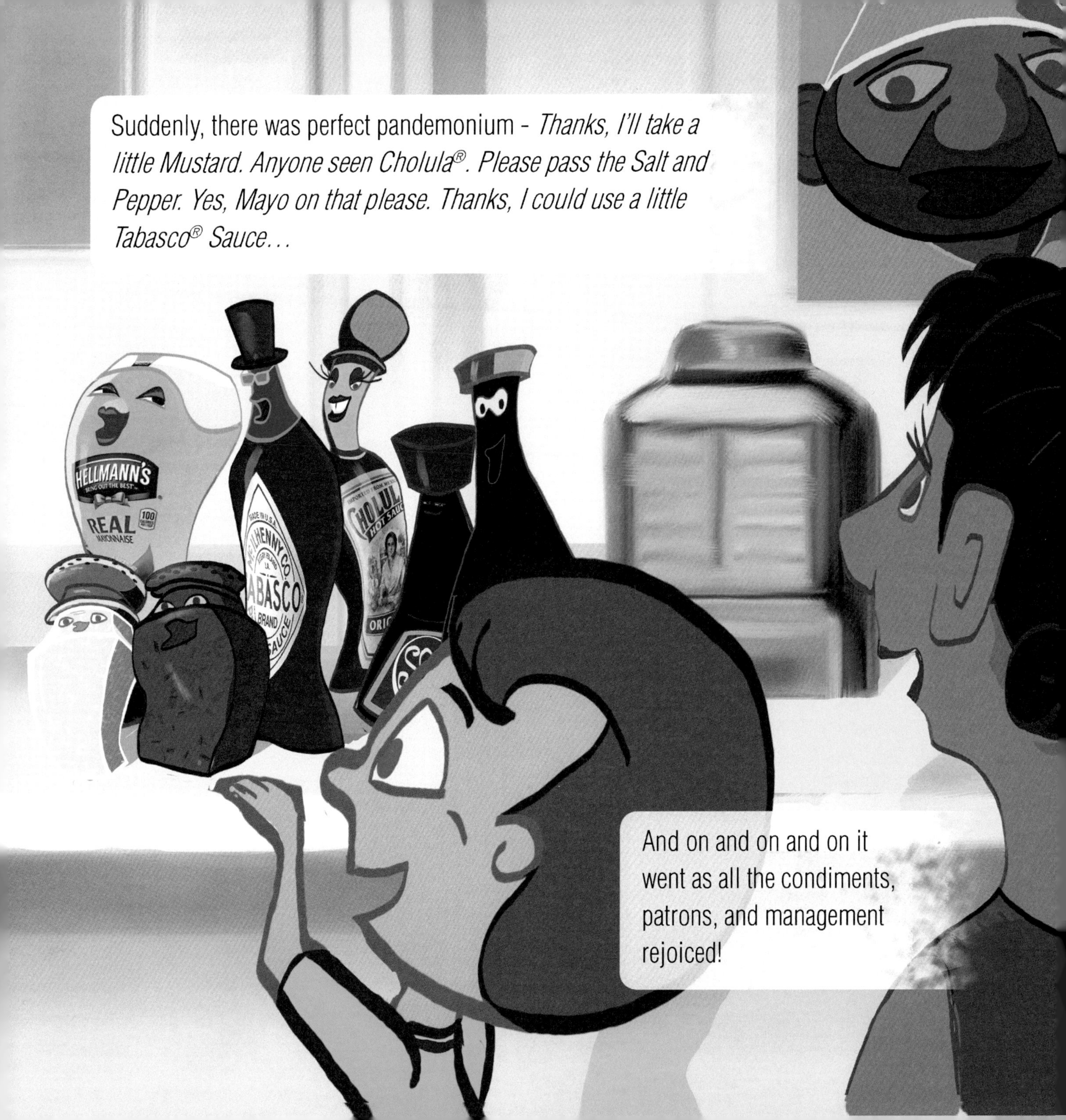
HELLMANN'S
REAL
MAYONNAISE

And on and on and on it went as all the condiments, patrons, and management rejoiced!

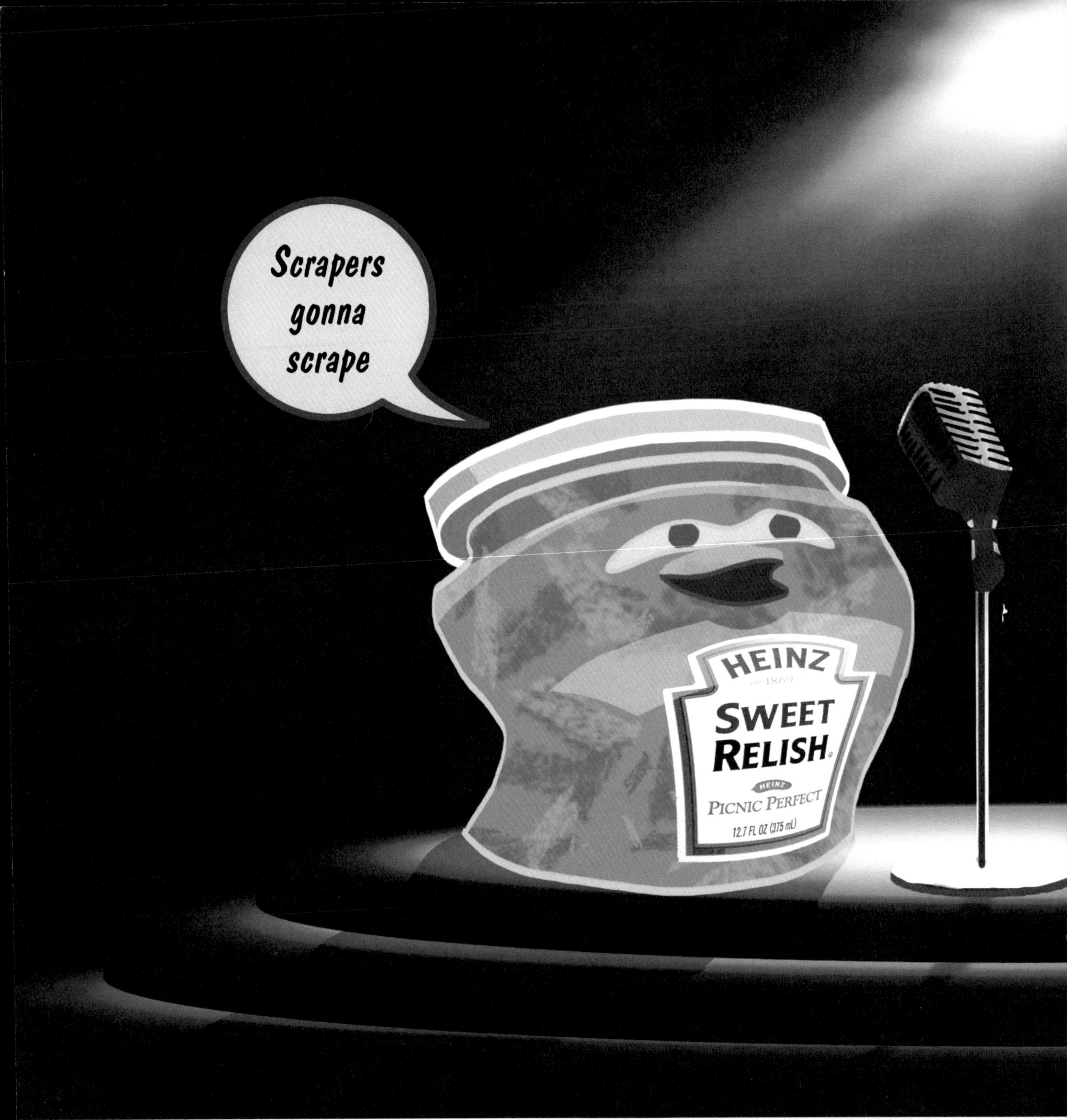
Scrapers gonna scrape
HEINZ
SWEET RELISH
PICNIC PERFECT
12.7 FL OZ (375 mL)

HELLMANN'S
"BRING OUT THE BEST"
REAL
MAYONNAISE
Haters gonna hate
Shake it off,
Shake it off

THE
CONDIMENT CHRONICLES
The Family Portrait

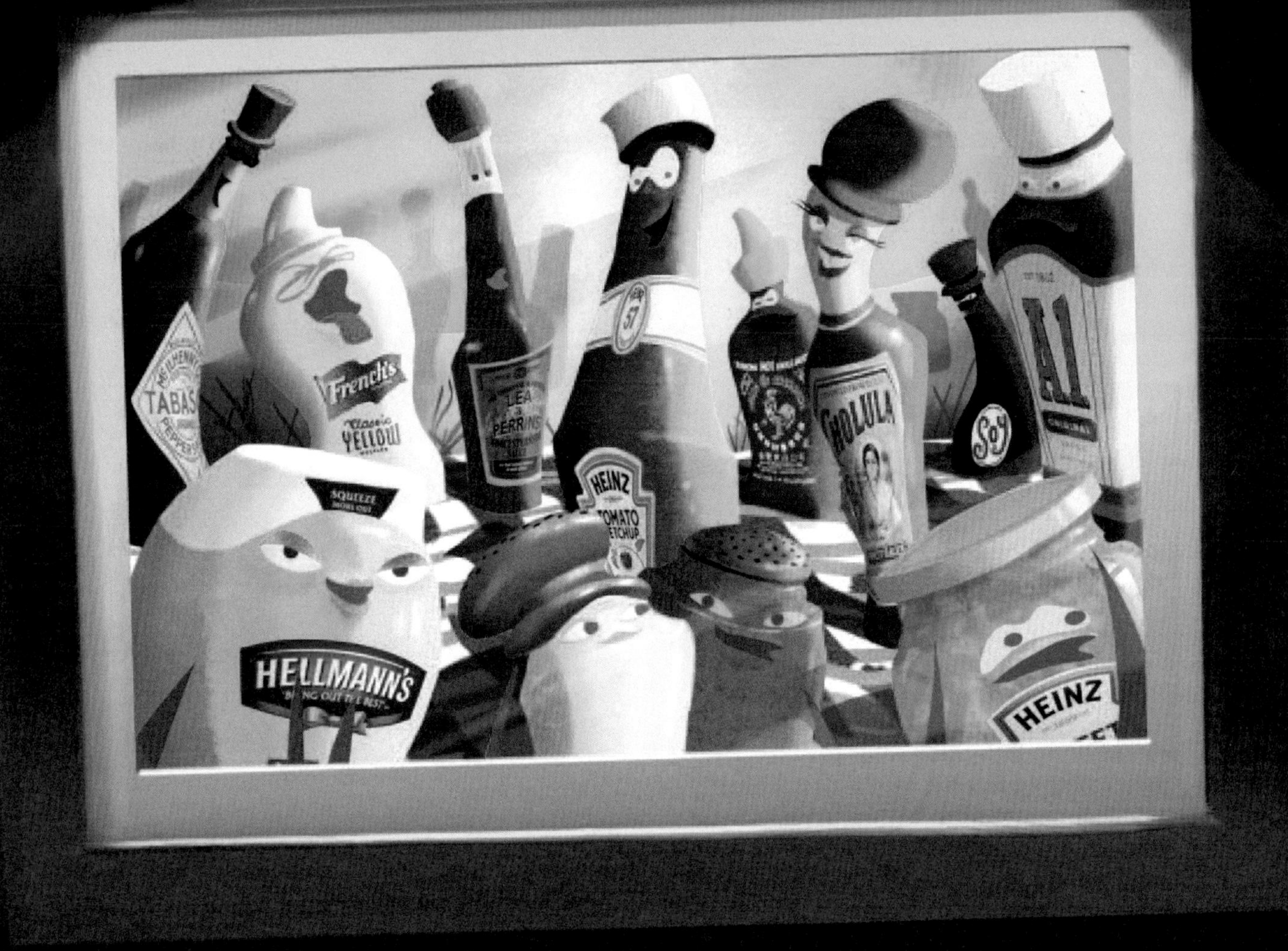
French's
Classic YELLOW
LEA PERRINS
57
HEINZ
SQUEEZE
HELLMANN'S
HEINZ
A1
SOY

In the beginning there were condiments
and the condiments thrived and conceived new condiments
and creativity abounded throughout the world.
Perhaps it started with...

SALT

(sal in Latin)

Salt is an essential mineral our body needs in order to function efficiently. Without realizing it, the early cave families satisfied their daily Salt requirement with the blood they consumed from the animals they ate; a necessary meal for well being and survival.

Who would have thought how important Salt was and is to our daily life!

Folk lore suggests many thousands of years ago the ancient Chinese were the first to know the effects of Salt in one's diet. By realizing its importance they gave it a monetary value and imposed a Salt tax on the population. This was an early glimpse of how civilizations placed monetary values, not only on Salt, but on future spices to come.[1]

As mankind became more civilized by cultivating farmland and raising animals, the value of Salt continued to increase. Recognizing its untold value as a seasoning, a medicine to aid with infection, and a preservative for meats and fish, the Romans of ancient times seized the opportunity and became the biggest producers. They created Salt by evaporating the water from Salt ponds along the Adriatic Sea (de sal inization).

Salt, often referred to as "white gold", was so valued that the Romans controlled the availability and the price. It was used as a form of money to pay their soldiers (sal aries) and a source of income for funding their wars.

Can you imagine getting a handful of Salt for doing your chores?

Preserving food with Salt allowed civilizations to travel, discover distant lands, and experience new spices and condiments. With ships travelling for months across many oceans, as did Christopher Columbus in 1492, sailors could then survive long voyages with preserved food stored on board (salted fish, meats, and pork).

Salt also became an important symbol representing purity and eternity. It was often used in baptismal and burial rites for keeping away evil spirits.[2]

Salt was and is an important commodity for all countries and people. She is the mother of all spices and condiments.

In the years to follow she developed a very close relationship with the spice of her life:

BLACK PEPPER

(Piper nigrum - Latin for the Black Pepper berry originating on the southwest coast of India)

Black Pepper, a wild growing vine, goes back to prehistoric times. In India, as early as 2000 BC, Pepper was known to be a very expensive spice cultivated and used regularly by the wealthy for seasoning their food. It was also thought to be used as a medicine to cure constipation, earaches, gangrene, and heart disease.[3]

Throughout the ages it became a prized item leading the way in the spice trade. Finding new homes and great acceptance in the Middle East, Europe, and Africa, Black Pepper's importance and value increased to such a level it came to be known as "black gold" and The King of spices along the trade routes.

If Pepper is "The King" it would only seem fitting that Salt must be "The Queen".

In Rome the Black Pepper berry became so valued for its taste and medicinal purposes it was accepted as currency just like Salt. During medieval times with Italy in control of most of the Pepper trade, this spice was known throughout Europe as a luxury item. As many countries became frustrated with Italy regulating the prices, they found their own trade routes to transport it home. Even Christopher Columbus went in search of riches and pepper berries. As history relates, he unfortunately brought back a chile pepper instead of the treasured Black Pepper berry.[4]

An unfortunate mistake for Columbus but his chile peppers may have helped in the creation of future condiments!

As time went on prices came down and Pepper, as is also true of Salt, became more available to all people. Both Salt and Pepper grew in popularity as many condiments were conceived by blending Salt and/or Pepper with other ingredients.

Salt and Pepper made for such a perfect couple for so many years. It wasn't until the late 1700's when Louis XVI recognized this and allowed only these two condiments, along with Parsley, to season his food.[5]

And so these two condiments with so much in common over a vast number of years sit side-by-side in a perfect union and have remained that way until today. We are reminded almost daily of their union when we hear the words:

Please pass the Salt and Pepper.

With Salt and Pepper establishing the family line it is easy to see how their "good tastes" have influenced future generations of condiments. One very popular offspring which is found in almost 97% of all homes in the U.S. and sold in over 140 countries is:

KETCHUP

In southern China around 300BC a preserved fish sauce called Koe-cheup (made from fish entrails, meat byproducts, and soybeans) was created.

Over many, many years this recipe evolved into an unpleasant smelling fish sauce called Ke-tchup: a base made of red rice wine, salted and fermented anchovies, and assorted spices which included Salt, Pepper, and Mustard.[6]

Ke-tchup for your hamburger and fries? Yuck…no thanks!

In the 1600's in search of spices and trade the Dutch and British travelled to Southeast Asia. Having been exposed to many different foods and spices, they developed a liking for the pungent fish sauce.

By the 1800's, to avoid travelling the long distances to transport this sauce, the British realized it would be cheaper and easier to create their own. Using the anchovy base they continued to develop a variety of sauces to complement many dishes.[7]

In 1812 the first sighting of the all important ingredient "tomato" appeared in a recipe published by a scientist from Philadelphia. The recipe continued to evolve and vinegar was added as a preservative. It wasn't until the 1870's that Henry Heinz fine tuned the recipe by dropping the fermented anchovy and adding additional Sugar to lengthen the time for preservation. This process created the sweet and sour taste of Ketchup as we know it today.[8]

Hallelujah! … Please pass the Ketchup!

Another favorite condiment, recorded very early in history, often "seated" next to Ketchup is:

MUSTARD

(Derived from the Latin word mustum - the fermented wine used to mix with the ground Mustard seed)

In India, as far back as 3000 BC, Mustard was often found growing in the wild. Through the ages it became a cultivated crop used for spicing food. Evolving into the 5th century BC the Greeks used it as a spice as well as a medicine (thanks to the Greek physician Hippocrates). By crushing the mustard seed and creating a moist wrap (mustard plaster) it was placed on sore muscles or aching backs to draw toxins from the body and relieve aches and pains.

As the Romans developed a great liking for Mustard as a spice and a medicine they looked to increase production. They travelled in and around France to have the monks in the local areas grow mustard plants alongside their wine crops. From the 9th century up through the 13th century Mustard became even more popular and profitable.

Realizing its potential and acting on his personal love of mustard, Pope John XXII of Avignon (1249-1334) created a new job in Dijon for his nephew. He whimsically titled him "Grand Moutardier du Pape": translated Grand Mustard-Maker to the Pope.

The rest is history.

In 1777 Mustard became so important to the town of Dijon that two townsmen, Maurice Grey and Antoine Poupon, created one of the most popular and "elite" Mustards of all time – Grey Poupon.

New recipes and variations followed on a regular basis.

In England in 1814 Jeremiah Colman introduced a powdered Mustard. Then in 1904 in the U.S. George and Francis French introduced French's® Classic Yellow Mustard at the St. Louis World's Fair. [9] By partnering with the hot dog French's® quickly grew to be the number one and all-time favorite Mustard in North America with distribution ongoing in more than 55 counties around the world.[10] Now…

100 years later the competition begins. Hot dogs have never had so many options!

Through the years sweet, spicy, hot, and grainy varieties of Mustard continue arriving into the mix. With its popularity growing Mustard has been known to partner with other well know peers. One such controversial condiment, much beloved by some and absolutely hated by others, is:

It is thought this creamy sauce, originally made with eggs and olive oil, may have been used by ancient Egyptians and Romans. Much later in the 18th century the French and the Spanish each declared that they were the original creator of Mayonnaise.[11]

The French claimed that in 1756 after the Duke de Richelieu defeated the British at the Port of Mahon (a city on the Spanish Island of Minorca in the Mediterranean Sea) his private chef prepared a victory meal using a traditional sauce made of egg yolks, cream, Salt, and spices. However, not finding any cream in the pantry, he substituted with oil,

blended his sauce, and named his creation Mahonnaise in honor of the special occasion
(victory at the Port of Mahon).

By the early 19th century this French recipe of Mayonnaise found its way into many British and German cookbooks. Immigrants coming to the United States brought these recipes with them and Mayonnaise, as we know it today, was ready to be formally introduced as a condiment into the U.S. market.[12]

It has been suggested that in 1910 in New York City a German immigrant by the name of Nina Hellmann prepared a creamy sauce for her husband's new deli. Known as Hellmann's® Mayonnaise, it became such a success Richard Hellmann started bottling and distributing this popular condiment from NY to as far west as the Rockies.

In 1932 Best Foods, a large west coast manufacturer of a very similar Mayonnaise, bought Hellmann's and continued to market and distribute both condiments. To this day these well-known branded names, now owned by Unilever, have stayed the same in each region so as not to confuse their loyal customers.[13]

Mayonnaise is used today in all types of hot and cold recipes, sandwich making, as well as "hooking" up with other condiments such as Ketchup (combined to make thousand island dressing) and Relish (creating creamy tartar sauce). Her reputation comes with devoted followers that love her creamy flavor; but there are also those that hate her with a passion and fervently yell out:

"Hold the Mayo!"

The creation of new condiments from the earliest times continued to grow and evolve at a steady pace. Over the ages it was evident that any condiment creating a flavorful taste experience was greatly prized and often developed into a commercial success. One of these flavor-filled condiments developed through traditional farming methods and perhaps named after the Old French word "relais" or the Middle English word "relis" (both meaning remainder) is:

RELISH

In the 18th century the condiment known as Relish began as a coarsely chopped fruit and/or vegetable that was cooked, pickled, and preserved. With no fresh produce available during the winter months and remnants left in the fields and gardens, preserving and preparing Relishes became very popular. Their flavors gave a bold new taste that complimented many a dish that was served.

Today in the U.S. there exist many versions of Relishes; some sweet and some sour. One sweet Relish, created in 1869 by the H.J. Heinz Company® is made from pickled cucumbers, vinegar, and Sugar.[14] Often seen at many a ball game as an added condiment for hot dogs and hamburgers, Relish sadly takes a back seat to the two favorites - Ketchup and Mustard.

Another condiment to reach commercial success was created in England in the early 1800's during the reign of King George IV. It was the King's chef who created this highly prized condiment which by 1862 was marketed as:

A.1.® SAUCE

For the first 100 years it was sold as a high quality multi-purpose condiment; a step above its relative Ketchup (both made from a tomato and vinegar base). Initially it was branded as a sauce to enhance the flavor for a variety of fish, meats, and vegetables; however, by 1960 it was rebranded as A.1.® Steak Sauce and marketed as a condiment for beef products.

By 2014, with consumer interest growing for all types of sauces, A.1.® Steak Sauce developed a new strategy for covering "more territory" ... not just beef. In search of new partners such as pork, fish, chicken, vegetables, fries, and more it was rebranded once again back to its original A.1.® Sauce roots as a multi-purpose condiment for all types of foods.[15]

As seen with A.1.® Sauce, creativity, including re-working recipes and rebranding, abounded through the ages with the desire to complement many a dish with a sweet, spicy, savory, or hot taste.

In the 1800's one such condiment, discovered in a foreign land and linked to The Family Tree of Condiments, was brought to England, modified, and reworked. It eventually found its way into many kitchens throughout Europe and was known as:

WORCESTERSHIRE SAUCE

Lord Sandys, a nobleman from Worcester England, discovered a savory sauce while travelling in Bengal, India. He liked the taste so much he found two chemists, John Lea and William Perrins, to re-create the recipe.

The two developed a sauce but unfortunately the taste was so bad they left it in jars abandoned in their basement. Several years went by before they discovered the forgotten jars. Giving it a taste-test, they were pleasantly surprised their recipe had distilled into a very savory sauce worth reviving. Bottling their creation, they began selling Lea & Perrins® Worcestershire Sauce commercially throughout Europe. By 1839 it was exported and distributed into the United States. Today it sells in over 130 countries worldwide. [16]

This very secret sauce containing anchovies and Salt is aged over time to develop its smooth flavor. Could this have originated from the fish sauce Koe-cheup and would that not make Worcestershire a relative of Ketchup as well as another very popular and widely used condiment known as:

 # SOY SAUCE

Today, who would think Soy Sauce, beginning its journey in China during prehistoric times, could possibly be related to Ketchup?

In ancient times fish and meats were preserved by packing them in Salt. Liquid drained from this procedure was then used as a seasoning for broths and sauces. The results of this process appear to be very similar to the original fish sauce called Koe-cheup. It was at this juncture that perhaps Ketchup and Soy Sauce each took a different path.

In the sixth century the Buddhist monks, being vegetarians, felt the need to create a meatless seasoning. By salting and fermenting grains, which included wheat and soybeans, they were the first to create the beginnings of a sauce similar to the Soy Sauce as we know it today.

Continuing its evolution, history suggests a Japanese priest studying in China brought this recipe back to Japan. He continued working on the taste to give it a mellow flavor to complement meat and fish dishes.

In the 17th century it is said that Maki Shige, wife of a Japanese warrior, taught herself how to make this Soy Sauce (thought to be the original Kikkoman® Soy Sauce recipe) and created the first Soy Sauce brewery.[17]

As history reveals everyone loves a new taste sensation and so the news of Soy Sauce spread throughout the world. Today it is used to enhance all types of foods: stir-fries, meats, poultry, fish, vegetables, pasta, and even ice cream!

Then there is Soy Sauce's closest relative:

TERIYAKI SAUCE

Teriyaki Sauce, a direct relative of Soy Sauce, was thought to have been conceived in the 17th century in Japan; however, there are no records to verify this origin. It appears to be a product created in the late 1800's when Japanese immigrants arrived in Hawaii. By mixing pineapple juice with Soy Sauce they created Teriyaki Sauce (teriyaki is also a cooking style - "teri" in Japanese means shine and "yaki" means grilled or broiled). Known widely as a marinating sauce, Teriyaki Sauce is also seated on the table as a dipping sauce.[18]

The Family Condiment Tree shows Teriyaki Sauce related to Soy Sauce and Soy Sauce related to Ketchup. All three seem to trace back to the same pungent fish sauce - Koe-cheup.

"Six degrees of separation"
If we look long and hard enough we will find, to some degree, we are all related!

Does this mean that the age-old Black Pepper berry is related to the red chile pepper found in:

TABASCO® BRAND PEPPER SAUCE

Making for one of the hottest condiments, some claim the chile peppers (named for the state of Tabasco, Mexico) arrived in the U.S. by 1848, right after the Mexican-American War. While waiting to be sent back to the U.S. the soldiers had time to collect souvenirs and sample the foods. As seen with many condiments from far off countries mankind is always on the lookout for new spices, tastes, or crops to grow. It was thought that soldiers returning to their homes in New Orleans may have brought back samples of this potent red chile pepper to share with family and friends.

Likewise, some say that Edmund McIlhenny, married to Mary Eliza Avery and living on Avery Island, Louisiana (known for its Sugar plantation and large Salt deposits), may have received red pepper seeds from a friend returning from the Mexican-American War. The loosely woven family story relates that in the 1860's he planted these seeds in the Avery family garden for their personal use; he was a banker not a farmer.

The Civil War came and the family fled the island. Upon their return after the war the chile pepper plants were found to have survived and represented a new business opportunity.

In 1868, after experimenting with recipes using the chile pepper, McIlhenny planted seeds and produced his first commercial crop. The following year he bottled his recipe in cologne bottles and sent them off as samples to wholesalers. The recipe of crushed and mashed red chile peppers, fermented in barrels covered in Salt, diluted with white wine vinegar from France, and then strained and prepared for bottling, became a great commercial success.

Trademarked by McIlhenny Company, Tabasco® brand Pepper Sauce is one of the most popular and well known hot sauces on the market today. Available in over 185 countries it is widely used to add taste and "heat" to a variety of foods from scrambled eggs, tomato juice, and soups to meats and fish.[19]

Tabasco® brand Pepper Sauce has many, many close relatives vying over the title for "Best Hot Sauce". The market is always wide open for new entries from around the world to join in this heated competition of:

 # HOT SAUCES

While the red chile pepper used in Tabasco® Sauce is very famous, there are over 140 types of chiles with varying degrees of "heat" grown in Mexico alone. Chiles are not related to the Black Pepper berry from India; they are a member of the tomato family (a fruit originating from Central and South America).[20]

Once again, welcome to the family ... hot sauces are distant relatives of Ketchup!

It was thought that chiles originated in Southern Mexico around 7000BC. By 3500 BC they were grown in Central and South America as crops for spices as well as for medicinal purposes (just like Salt, Black Pepper and Mustard). As with all relatives, chiles come in many sizes, shapes, colors, and the all important "units of heat" as measured on the Scoville Heat Scale. Chiles, prized for their heat and flavor, have travelled the world to be grown and used in the creation of many new condiments.[21]

The popular 100 year old Cholula® Hot Sauce, a recipe conceived in Chapala, Jalisco, Mexico, is distributed throughout North America. In California in 1971 Mexican immigrants from Guadalajara, Jalisco created Tapatio® Hot Sauce; another favorite condiment widely distributed in the U.S. as well as other countries worldwide.

In 1980 in Los Angeles Sriracha Hot Chili Sauce, a "secret" sauce made of red jalapeno chile peppers, was introduced by David Tran, the founder of Huy Fong Foods. Through the years the increased popularity of this multi-use hot sauce has created a growing worldwide fire storm of enthusiastic followers; a condiment many cannot live without. (Sriracha is thought to have originated from Sriraja Panich Sauce; created in 1949 in Si Racha Thailand.)

Hot Condiment Flash ... Let the games begin!

The family tree is constantly growing with new relatives conceived on a daily basis!

As a result of travelers collecting spices and herbs throughout the ages, a multitude of condiments have arrived at the counter ... and the table. Staying current with the times, the family of condiments continues to evolve: new combinations as well as new recipes including organic, gluten free, less sugar, and less salt.

Condiments are everywhere: found in every household, restaurant, diner, sports venue, camp ground, and more (a packet of Ketchup or hot sauce might be found in the glove compartment of a car!). There are condiment cook books, condiment challenges, condiment races, condiment costumes, condiment songs, condiment comedy, condiment clubs, and more.

Condiments inspire creativity.

It's all about experimentation and forever blending spices and condiments together to develop new taste sensations that mankind loves and sometimes feels it can't live without.

So ...

"Bring em back, bring em back!" he begged the management. "It's just not the same without them.

We need them. We need them all!" he sobbed.

A life without condiments would be colorless and bland! Thankful are we for each and every one.
Amen!

DIFFERENCE BETWEEN A SPICE AND A CONDIMENT:

- A spice is used in the preparation of food.

- A condiment can be a spice or a sauce "seated" at the table for each individual to enhance the flavor of food to his or her personal liking.[22]

- to condiment : verb 1. action of adding condiments to your food. I like to condiment my hamburger and fries with Ketchup. (verb not found in any dictionary)

- condimentour : noun 1. a person who applies condiments to his/her food or another's (warning: Do at your own risk!). I am the condimentour of my own food. 2. a person who creates condiments. (noun not found in any dictionary)

[1] http://www.saltworks.us/salt_info/si_HistoryOfSalt.asp

[2] http://www.himalayancrystalsalt.com/salt-history.html

[3] http://www.lifescript.com/food/articles/t/the_storied_origins_of_black_pepper.aspx

[4] http://www.history.com/news/hungry-history/off-the-spice-rack-the-story-of-pepper

[5] http://gizmodo.com/how-salt-and-pepper-became-the-yin-and-yang-of-condimen-1258049326 Andrew Tarantola 10/8/13

[6] http://www.history.com/news/hungry-history/ketchup-a-saucy-history July 20, 2012 Ketchup: A Saucy History By Stephanie Butler

[7] http://www.slate.com/articles/life/food/2012/05/ketchup_s_chinese_origins By Dan Jurafsky

[8] http://www.npr.org/blogs/codeswitch/2013/12/02/248195661/ketchup-the-all-american-condiment-that-comes-from-asia December 03, 2013 Lakshmi Gandhi

[9] http://www.thenibble.com/reviews/main/condiments/history-of-mustard.asp The History Of Mustard · Victoria Marshman - The Nibble - October 2008.

[10] https://www.rb.com/media-investors/category-performance/food

[11] The Nibble http://www.thenibble.com/reviews/main/cheese/eggs/mayonnaise-history.asp The History Of Mayonnaise KAREN HOCHMAN - The Nibble - August 2010.

[12] http://www.slate.com/blogs/browbeat/2013/12/27/mayonnaise_history_was_it_invented_by_the_french_or_the_spanish.html By David Merritt Johns Slate's Culture Blog Dec. 27 2013 1:06 PM

[13] The Nibble http://www.thenibble.com/reviews/main/cheese/eggs/mayonnaise-history.asp The History Of Mayonnaise KAREN HOCHMAN - The Nibble - August 2010.

[14] http://powerfulpierre.hubpages.com/hub/Everything-You-Always-Wanted-to-know-about-RELISH Powerful Pierre, HubPages Author February 9, 2014

[15] http://newscenter.kraftfoodsgroup.com/phoenix.zhtml?c=253200&p=irol-newsArticle&ID=1931607 NORTHFIELD, III., May 15, 2014 /PRNewswire

[16] http://www.leaperrins.com/history.aspx

[17] http://www.kikkomanusa.com/foodservice/soysaucebasics/storyofsoysauce.php http://www.madehow.com/Volume-3/Soy-Sauce.html

[18] http://www.ehow.com/about_5251710_history-teriyaki-sauce.html http://www.teriyakisalmon.org/history-of-teriyaki-sauce/

[19] Shane K. Bernard, Ph.D.'s Tabasco: An Illustrated History (Avery Island, La.: McIlhenny Company, 2007)

[20] http://www.cosmicchile.com/xdpy/kb/chile-pepper-history.html

[21] http://kitchenproject.com/history/HotSauce/ http://www.hotsauce101.com/wilbur-scoville.html

[22] http://www.latinbag.com/index.php/es/blog/item/32-difference-between-spices-and-condiments

S.H.Wood, author of the humorous children's book *The Condiment Chronicles ... Please Pass the Ketchup*, is a huge fan of Mayo and proud to admit it. A meal without condiments is like a garden without flowers: "It's just not right!"

She lives in Northern California with her husband Chris and their Shih Tzu, Lilli. Two beautiful daughters, Meghan and Liza have been her biggest supporters. This is her first picture book.

Visit her any time at:
www.shwoodtheauthor.com
shwoodtheauthor@gmail.com
S.H. Wood Author (Facebook)

Nic Gregory, is an Australian born artist now living in Los Angeles. With a love of animation and art, Nic has travelled across the globe to achieve his artistic dreams. Lifelong creative passions have allowed him to illustrate books, exhibit his original pastels and work in the LA animation industry.

With his wife Amy by his side, Nic has made a successful move to America and looks to continue his drive to produce appealing art that inspires books, animation and games. You can follow Nic's journey in the art world or contact him at:

www.nicgregory.com
nic@nicgregory.com
Nic_XL (Twitter)
nicgregoryart (Instagram)
Nic Gregory (Facebook)

A meal without condiments would be colorless and bland!

Thankful are we for each and every one.

68269480R00033

Made in the USA
Lexington, KY
06 October 2017